CRAFTING

Lamps
&
Shades

JODIE DAVIS

krause publications

700 East State St., Iola, WI 54990-0001
Telephone (715) 445-2214

Please call or write for our free catalog of publications. Our toll-free number to place an order or obtain a free catalog is 800-258-0929 or please use our regular business telephone 715-445-2214 for editorial comment and further information.

While all care is taken to provide the reader with knowledge of the safety precautions relating to the use of the materials featured in this book, the Publisher cannot take responsibility for personal injury or accident which may occur while working with the materials. Please carefully read all manufacturer's instructions regarding the safe use of materials and equipment before beginning work.

Photography by Ross Hubbard
Book design by Jan Wojtech
Manufactured in the United States of America

Library of Congress Cataloging-In-Publication Data

Davis, Jodie
        Crafting lamps & shades
        1. crafts   2. lamp making   3. home decorating

ISBN 0-87341-661-9

                                        98-84097
                                        CIP

Acknowledgments

Thanks to all of the suppliers listed in the Sources section who so generously supplied me with materials, guidance, and encouragement. While I worked on the book, the UPS man made many trips to my door bringing goodies from far and wide. It was like Christmas!

And special thanks to Barbara Hennig, who more than once throughout the years we've done books together, has called or e-mailed when stuck on an illustration and said, "I know the illustration will make the text obvious, but I have to illustrate it and all I have is the manuscript. Help!"

Table of *Contents*

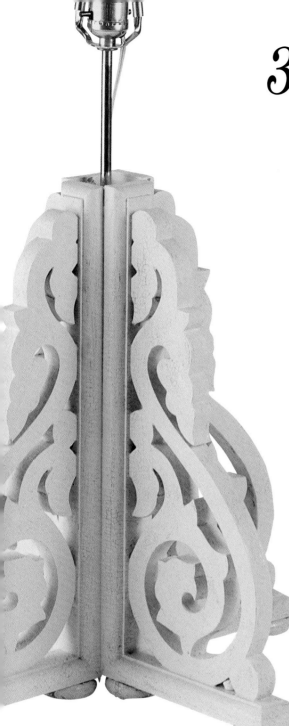

3 PROJECTS - 24

Introduction

The trick to home
decorating today is making it personal.

Whether your decorating taste runs country, contemporary, ethnic, or is an eclectic mix, giving it the stamp of your personality is what makes your house your home.

After the paint, wallpaper, floor covering, and furniture are in place, the true pulse of a room is dictated by those touches that are added one-by-one with careful thought. That's where lamps come in. Yes, you can set that plain brass candlestick lamp on your end table. But it says nothing about you. Wouldn't you rather select something that reflects your personality? And wouldn't it really speak "you" if you made it?

Crafting Lamps & Shades presents ten lamps and 20 shades to help you create your own decorative "just so's." Lest you think these projects are difficult, know that I do not consider myself an expert in any of the skills used to make the lamps. Yes, I have written many crafts books, but until now, all in the fiber arts field. So, yes, I am a professional designer, but as for painting and working with a drill, well, let's say I learned by doing.

In fact, that's part of the fun of making these projects. They offer the excuse to delve into the worlds of rubber stamping, dried flowers, stenciling, and—one of my favorite pastimes—"junking!" Join me!

Jodie Davis

1

*L*amp Making Primer

You don't need to be a master electrician to make lamps. All you need to know is which wire goes with which of two screws on a socket. Nor do you need special tools. A screwdriver is the only tool I needed to wire the lamps pictured in this book. That's right, wiring is as simple as turning two screws!

We'll start with a *Gray's Anatomy* of a lamp, then introduce you to the components used to make lamps. Next up, I'll show you how to wire a lamp. Then we'll jump right into a bare bones lamp that will show you how simple it is to make a lamp from scratch. Let's get started!

ANATOMY OF A LAMP

The basic anatomy of a lamp is diagrammed here. With only a few minor variations, all the lamps in this book are constructed this way.

GUIDE TO LAMP PARTS

You are probably familiar with many, if not all, of the components that make up a lamp. Following is a description of each of them. This will help you attach a name to them so you'll know what I'm talking about when you run across them in project instructions and materials lists.

socket shell

cardboard insulating sleeve

socket core with terminal screws and on/off knob

underwriter's knot

socket cap

lamp pipe

cord

SOCKETS

The down-to-business component of lamps, sockets come in several varieties. In choosing a socket, ask yourself how you want to turn the lamp on and off and how you want to route the cord.

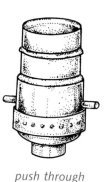

push through

pull chain

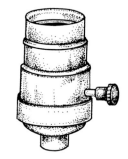

turn on/off

As for the on/off question, sockets come with either a key, a pull chain, or a knob. The first two choices offer simple on/off operation. The knob can provide a three-way intensity setting when used with a three-way bulb.

The cord routing question is dictated by the lamp itself. To illustrate this, consider two lamps. The first is the Basic Lamp shown. A hole has been drilled in the center of the bottom of the salad bowl base (which, because I turned the salad bowl over to make the base of the lamp, is the top of the lamp base) and a smaller hole has been drilled in the side of the salad bowl. The cord comes down from the socket, through the lamp pipe, into the bowl of the salad bowl, and out the hole in the side of the bowl.

Now, consider the Vase Lamp. I couldn't bear the thought of drilling a hole in the side of that lovely Italian art deco vase, so I used a side-exit socket. The cord is wired into the socket through a hole in the side of the socket. Sure, the wire is obvious on the outside of the lamp, but hopefully the lamp won't be viewed from all sides so the wire can be hidden at the back of the lamp.

To remove the guesswork, I have designated whether you will need a bottom or side outlet socket for each project in the book. You may choose between the switch options.

Lamp Pipe

Simply a hollow pipe 3/8" in diameter, lamp pipe comes in lengths ranging from 6" to 18" in 1" increments. Both ends are pre-threaded and the finish is brass.

Nuts and Washers

Lamp suppliers carry nuts and lock washers made specifically to fit lamp pipes. Where nuts will show on the finished lamps, you will find hardware pretty enough to be seen.

Finial Hardware

Little threaded plugs are available from lamp making suppliers to turn most anything into a finial.

Vase Caps

Vase caps cover the opening at the top of a vase, such as on the Vase Lamp. A hole in the center is just the right size for the lamp pipe to fit through.

Harp

The harp is the apparatus that holds a shade above the light bulb. In reality, a harp consists of two parts, though the nomenclature doesn't suggest this. First is the harp wing piece that goes below the socket on the lamp pipe and has to be held in place by something such as a nut below it. The harp wing piece allows removal of the top piece of the harp when the lamp is fully constructed. This is a nice feature for many reasons, including boxing up lamps to move them, or to change the size of the harp itself to accommodate a new, smaller, or larger shade.

The piece called the harp is attached to the harp wings by squeezing the two "arms" of the harp together to fit them inside the grooves at the inside of the harp wings. The pressure holds it all in place, as do two helpful little clips that fall neatly into place. Check one out and you'll see how simple and well-conceived a device a harp is.

Harps come in many heights so you can adjust the harp according to the requirements of a particular lamp and shade marriage.

The alternative to a harp is a shade constructed from a "bulb clip" shade frame that clips directly to the bulb. In this case, no harp is required. More on this in the shade section.

For each of the projects in this book, I designate what I used for the particular lamp/shade combination.

CORD

I recommend purchasing cord sets for your lamp projects. You can purchase cords and plugs separately but unless you have a specific reason for doing so, buy the cord set with the plug already attached to the cord. This saves time and on many sets the raw wire at the other end of the cord is conveniently spliced, twisted, and neatly capped, ready for a quick and easy installation into the socket.

Cords sets are available in white, black, brown, and clear. Some suppliers offer a choice of lengths and an in-line on/off switch may be an option.

WIRING

In the months I've been working on this book, I've been asked more than a few times something along these lines, "Oh, you're making lamps *and wiring them too?*" I get the distinct impression fear of wiring, a.k.a. electricity, is quite common.

Such sentiment is totally unnecessary. In fact, wiring is the easiest step in making lamps. To prove this to yourself, read on and follow the process of making the Basic Lamp. At the end of the instructions I bet you'll say, "Is that all there is to it?"

Of course, when working with electricity, caution is mandatory. For lamp making, only two precautions need to be kept in mind. The first one is obvious: Never work on a lamp (or any other electrical appliance for that matter) when it is plugged in. You already knew that one, so let's go on. Second and last, memorize (better yet, I wrote it down in a prominent place because I have leaky brain syndrome) the cardinal

rule in hooking up cords to lamp sockets: The wide prong of the plug is the neutral side. The wire leading from the wide prong is either ribbed or marked with writing of some type and goes to the silver screw in the socket.

What does this mean? Examine a cord set. Note the plug. One prong is wider than the other. This is a polarized plug. You will also notice that the housing of the wire running from the wide prong is either ridged or has writing on it, whereas the other side does not. This unmarked wire is the hot wire which attaches to the brass screw in the socket. If you switch the wires during lamp assembly, the lamp may work but touch the socket and you'll be in for a shock. Literally! You have discovered polarity. When wired properly, the lamp switch interrupts the current-carrying hot wire so when the lamp is turned off, there is no power flowing through it. And no shocks.

So remember: The wide prong is neutral, the ribbed or marked wire goes to the silver screw.

A BASIC LAMP

Starting with a bare-bones lamp is a great way to understand the basics of lamp making. This lamp illustrates the variety of things you can do with a simple idea. To make this lamp, all you need is a base of some sort that you can put a hole in, a lamp pipe, a cord, a few nuts and washers, and a socket. Once the components are gathered, it takes all of a few minutes to assemble the lamp. The only tools required are an electric drill and a screwdriver. Have some sandpaper on hand in case the drilled hole requires neatening.

I used a teak salad bowl for my lamp base, but you can use anything you can drill a hole through.

SALAD BOWL BASIC LAMP

MATERIALS

- Wooden salad bowl
- Rubber grommet for cord hole (see Sources)
- Lamp pipe of desired length
- Bottom outlet socket
- Lamp harp
- Harp wings
- Cord set
- Three nuts
- One washer
- Electric drill with 3/8" and 1/4" drill bits
- Sandpaper

INSTRUCTIONS

1 Find and mark the exact center of the bowl. Since some bowls may have been well-used or are handmade, your bowl may not be exactly round. To find the center, I made a paper template of the bottom of the salad bowl then folded it in half and in half again. I made a hole at the center, aligned it again on the bottom of the salad bowl, and made a chalk mark through the hole onto the wood.

2 With the bowl upside-down, drill a 3/8" hole at the center mark. Clean up the hole with sandpaper.

3 With a 1/4" bit, drill a hole for the cord to emerge from the side of the bowl. Clean up the hole with sandpaper. Since my bowl was a bit tired-looking, I oiled it at this point and let it set.

4 Install the grommet. I had to pare mine down on one side to get it through the thick wall of the bowl. Glue it in place.

5 You may wish to spray paint your lamp pipe rather than keep it metallic. If so, use a solvent to remove any sealer on the pipe before spray painting. Or you may wish to put a length of copper pipe around the lamp pipe as I did. I bought a pipe cutter and cut mine to fit.

6 Screw a nut on one end of the lamp pipe and tighten it as far as it will go. From the bottom of the bowl, insert the end into the bowl. From inside the bowl, screw a washer and then a nut on the pipe. Tighten.

7 Set the bowl upside-down on your work surface so it is now what will be right-side-up for the lamp. Screw the remaining nut on the remaining threaded end of the pipe as far as it will go. If using a harp rather than a clip shade (see page 11), slide the harp wings onto the pipe. Screw the socket cap into place.

8 When wiring a lamp, think from the bottom up. Push the raw wire end of the lamp cord through the grommet into the inside of the salad bowl and up through the pipe.

9 Separating the two wires so you have enough length to do so, tie an Underwriters' knot in the cord.

10 Loosen the silver (neutral) terminal screw in the socket. Loop the bare ends of the marked or ridged wire clockwise and place it around the silver terminal screw. Tighten the screw.

11 Loosen the brass (hot) terminal screw. Form the remaining (unmarked side) wire into a loop and place it around the brass screw. Tighten the screw.

12 Slide the socket shell into place over the socket core. Snap into place.

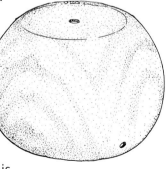

Shade making Primer

ANATOMY OF LAMPSHADES

Traditional lampshades start with a frame covered with either paper or fabric. One form of frame is simply two wire rings, most often round. Paper or fabric is adhered to a stiff material, namely styrene, and glued to the rings. Unbacked fabric shades need more support, so the fabric is attached to a one-piece rigid shade frame.

When using certain materials for shades, you will want to select low-wattage bulbs to prevent yellowing and degradation of materials due to heat. Handmade papers are susceptible, as are dried flowers. The manufacturer of the wooden shade recommends a low-wattage bulb intended for ceiling fans.

As discussed in the section devoted to lamp making parts, there are two choices for securing the shade to the lamp. Use of a harp, which is attached to the lamp itself, calls for washer top shades. If your lamp lacks a harp, you will want to choose a bulb clip style shade.

GUIDE TO PARTS AND SUPPLIES

All the supplies listed below are available from the lamp suppliers listed in the Sources section at the back of the book.

FITTER RINGS

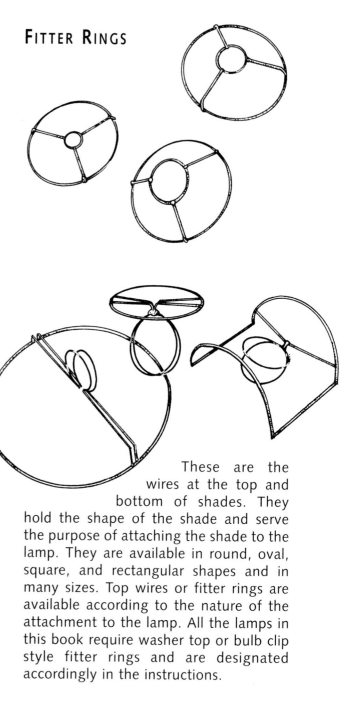

These are the wires at the top and bottom of shades. They hold the shape of the shade and serve the purpose of attaching the shade to the lamp. They are available in round, oval, square, and rectangular shapes and in many sizes. Top wires or fitter rings are available according to the nature of the attachment to the lamp. All the lamps in this book require washer top or bulb clip style fitter rings and are designated accordingly in the instructions.

SHADE FRAMES

These are complete frames with wires at top and bottom plus additional ribs to form complex shapes. Many are very fancy, used for highly decorative Victorian lampshades.

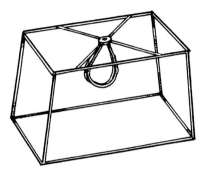

GLUE

Lampshade suppliers offer a water-soluble glue that dries quickly and clear. Unlike other glues that may offer these benefits, glue made specifically for shade making will not yellow. You may also want to try the inexpensive glue dispenser sold with the glue. It makes for pinpoint glue applications.

BINDING TAPE

Used to trim the shades, binding tape encases the raw edges of the styrene and paper and the top and bottom wires of the shade. It is glued on and makes a neat edge, ready for your trim. I prefer the 13/16"-wide cotton twill carried by The Lamp Shop. It makes easy work of creating a neat edging.

STYRENE

Styrene is a translucent material used as a support for lampshades constructed using fitter rings. Pressure-sensitive styrene has a sticky side which is covered with a peel-off paper. Decorative paper or fabric is easily applied to the adhesive side. I used this for many of the shades in the book.

PRESSURE-SENSITIVE FELT

Apply this product to the bottom of the lamp to protect the surface the lamp sits on.

BULLDOG CLIPS

Thanks to their wide jaws, bulldog clips hold glued shades together for drying. Be careful how you clamp them so they don't leave indentations. For clamping shade parts together to check fit, I use gentler clothespins.

HUG SNUG

This 100% rayon ribbon wrap is used to wrap lampshade frames in preparation for either glued or hand-sewn fabric covered shades.

DRAFTING A LAMPSHADE PATTERN

Now we turn to the actual skills used in making lampshades. For a lampshade using a top and bottom fitter ring, you will need a pattern in order to cut the styrene. Though at first glance this may look like geometry, you should have no trouble completing a pattern in 15 minutes.

Once you have determined the width at the top and bottom of the shade, as well as the height, you can draft the pattern for the shade.

MATERIALS

- *Sharp pencil*
- *Large piece of paper (brown craft paper on rolls works great)*
- *Scissors*
- *Yardstick*
- *Measuring tape*
- *Straight pins*

INSTRUCTIONS

1 Spread the paper on a large work surface. Starting at the bottom right of the paper, draw a straight, horizontal line (AB), equal in length to the diameter of the bottom ring of the shade.

2 Mark the exact center of this line. Mark this as point C. From C, draw a long line upwards and perpendicular to the AB line.

3 From C, measure the height of the shade upwards along the vertical line. Mark the end point D.

4 At point D, draw a line perpendicular to line CD and equal to the diameter of the top ring, placing the center of the line at D. Mark the end points E and F.

5 Draw a line through points A and E, extending it to intersect line CD. Mark this point X. Do the same for BF.

6 Place the end of the measuring tape with the hole at point B, centering the hole over the point. Place a pin in the tape at Point X. Put the tip of a pencil in the hole of the measuring tape. Slowly swing the tape in an arc from point B through point A and beyond, marking an arc with the pencil as you go.

7 Do the same for points F through E.

8 Placing the weld of the bottom ring at point B, carefully roll the ring along the drawn arc line from B to A and on until the weld meets the paper again. Mark that as point G.

9 Draw a line from point G to X.

10 Mark the intersection of the top ring arc and line GX as point H. Draw a line 1/2" above line GH. This will be the overlap at the back of the shade.

11 Carefully cut out the pattern. Test the pattern by temporarily attaching it to the rings with bulldog clips or clothespins.

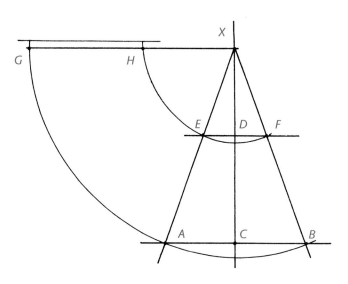

CONSTRUCTING A ROUND LAMPSHADE

Now that you have drafted your pattern, let's make a shade!

INSTRUCTIONS

❶ Lay the styrene paper-side-up on a clean work surface. Place the lampshade pattern on top. Weight the pattern to hold it in place. With a sharp pencil, carefully trace around the pattern onto the styrene.

❷ Remove the paper backing from the styrene. Apply the wrong side of the paper or fabric shade material to the sticky styrene. Start at one edge and work across. Often I find it easier to lay the fabric or paper on the tabletop wrong-side-up and stick the styrene to it from above.

❸ Carefully cut out the shade, just inside the pencil lines.

❹ Mark the 1/2" seam allowance on the wrong side of one end of the shade. Place a bead of glue inside this marked line. Butt the other end of the shade material to this, overlapping the ends. Clamp the top and bottom edges of the seam with bulldog clips. Clean up any glue seepage. Lay the shade down on a clean surface. Weight the seam with books and allow the glue to dry.

❺ When the glue has dried, remove the books and bulldog clips. Apply a thin bead of glue along the top inside edge of the shade, rotating the shade as you do so. Slip the top ring into the shade from the bottom. Fit the ring just inside the top edge. Clamp in place with a bulldog clip at the back seam. Work around the shade, matching the ring and clamping with clips. Clean up any extra glue with a moist towel.

❻ Turn the shade upside-down and repeat for the bottom ring.

❼ Allow to dry several hours or overnight and remove the bulldog clips.

WRAPPING A SHADE FRAME

In the instructions for several of the lamp-shades you will be directed to wrap a shade frame in preparation for the application of fabric. To do so, follow these steps.

MATERIALS

* Wire shade frame
* Hug Snug tape
* Glue

INSTRUCTIONS

❶ Begin at a joint where a vertical strut meets the top wire. Cut a piece of tape nearly three times longer than the strut. Wrap the tape over the top wire as shown. Leave the tail hanging.

❷ Wrap the Hug Snug tape at a sharp right angle around the top of the strut, covering the tail. Apply a small dot of glue at the back of the tape. Keep wrapping the tape around the strut, working your way down the strut, overlapping the tape as you go.

❸ When you reach the bottom wire, wrap the tape around the bottom wire a few times, then run it back through under itself. Secure with a scant drop of glue. Repeat for all the struts, then do the same for the top and bottom wires.

TRIMMING SHADES

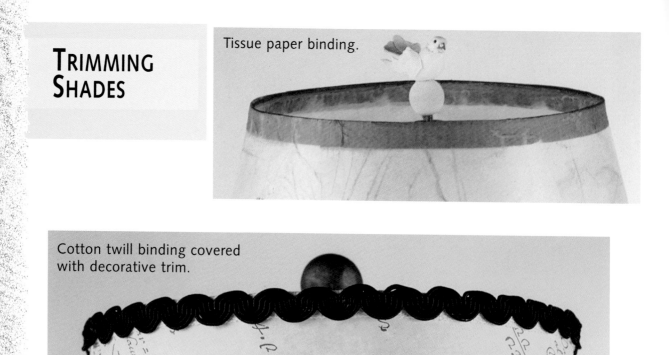

Tissue paper binding.

Cotton twill binding covered with decorative trim.

To finish your lampshade, trim the top and bottom edges with some sort of decorative trim. Rayon/polyester blend grosgrain ribbon in 5/8" width is the traditional choice. I particularly enjoy working with 13/16" cotton twill binding tape. Either of these encase the raw edge of the styrene and the fitter wire. In case of the cotton twill binding, I then apply a grosgrain ribbon or other trim over the twill binding tape.

To determine the amount of binding needed, refer to this chart. For a general rule of thumb, multiply the top and bottom ring diameters by four and add them together.

For more specific measurements for round shades:

Add the top and bottom ring amounts together and add 1" (2.5cm) for overlaps.

Ring Diameter	Circumference
4" (10cm)	13" (33cm)
5" (12.5cm)	17" (43cm)
6" (15cm)	20" (51cm)
7" (18cm)	23" (58.5cm)
8" (20.5cm)	26" (66cm)
9" (23cm)	29" (73.5cm)
10" (25.5cm)	32" (81.5cm)
11" (28cm)	36" (91.5cm)
12" (30.5cm)	39" (99cm)
13" (33cm)	42" (107cm)
14" (35.5cm)	45" (115cm)
15" (38cm)	49" (125cm)
16" (40.5cm)	52" (132cm)
17" (43cm)	55" (140cm)
18" (45.5cm)	59" (150cm)

INSTRUCTIONS

1 Draw a guideline with a drafting compass around the edge of the shade. To determine the measurement, hold the trim in place. Make sure there will be enough at the front and back once it goes around the curve to cover the edge of the wire/styrene.

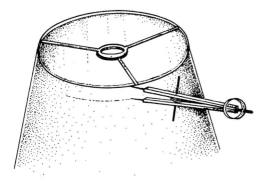

2 Straighten the beginning edge of the grosgrain or cotton twill binding by trimming along a rib.

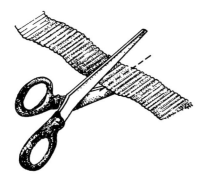

3 Apply a bead of glue to the first few inches of the binding along just one half of the binding as shown. Smooth with a paint brush.

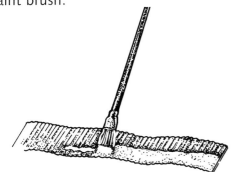

4 Starting at the back seam, apply the trim to the edge of the frame, just hiding the drawn guideline with the edge of the binding. Finger press in place. Allow the glue to set a minute.

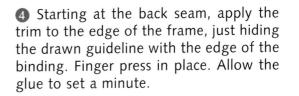

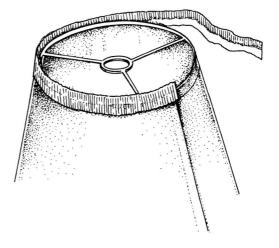

5 Working in approximate 6" increments, apply more glue to the binding and press it in place on the shade. When you reach the back seam, cut off the excess binding perpendicular to the back seam, overlapping the binding 1/4".

6 Apply a thin even coat of glue to the inside edge of the binding protruding from the top of the shade. Turn the binding to the inside of the shade, rolling it over the wire. Make slashes at the ribs of the fitter wire to allow the binding to fit neatly. Run a fingernail over the binding, under the wire to ensure a snug fit. Repeat for the other end of the shade. Set aside to dry.

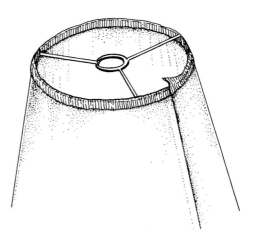

3 Projects

Bobbin/Trivet Lamp

*I*f scouting antique shops is your passion, you'll have fun finding the items to make this lamp. The wooden bobbin is fairly easy to find. The trivet can be old or new like the one here. Just be sure there's a hole on the center of the trivet wide enough to put the lamp pipe through.

This lamp is but a mere step up from the basic lamp in the previous section. Rather than use a salad bowl for a base, I used a wrought iron trivet. And I simply slipped a wooden bobbin over the lamp pipe. Easy!

The length of the lamp pipe will be determined by the height of your bobbin. Work through step three, using lamp pipe in the length of your best guess. Since they are inexpensive, I had a few on hand just in case. If the one you selected is too long or short, start over with another.

The lampshade on this lamp is made of handmade paper, following the instructions for constructing a round lampshade on page 20 and using the pattern on page 107. I used a different handmade paper in place of grosgrain ribbon or cotton twill binding to cover the tip and bottom wire/raw edges of the shade.

MATERIALS

- Wrought iron trivet
- Wooden bobbin
- Lamp pipe
- Two washers larger than the hole in the center of the trivet
- Two or three lamp nuts
- Two lamp washers
- Lamp neck
- Socket with bottom exit for cord
- Cord set
- Wrought iron black acrylic paint
- Harp wings
- Harp
- Finial

INSTRUCTIONS

Note: Go through these steps as a trial run before tightening everything. You can work with the placement of the nuts on the threaded ends of the pipe to get a proper fit.

❶ If there is a chance the large washers will show when the lamp is finished, spray paint them black. Mine is covered by the bottom of the bobbin, so I didn't have to paint it.

❷ Place a hexagonal nut on one end of the lamp pipe and then a small and a large washer. From the top of the trivet, insert the pipe into the hole in the center. From underneath the trivet, put the large washer then a small washer and a hexagonal lamp nut on the pipe and tighten.

❸ Slip the bobbin over the pipe. Place the neck over the top of the pipe. Slide the harp wings on. Screw the socket in place. Add a nut below it if necessary.

❹ Wire the lamp following the instructions for Wiring Basics on page 12. Install the harp.

❺ Spray paint the finial. Allow to dry. Install the shade. Screw on the finial.

Lighthouse/ Birdhouse Lamp

Drill a hole, do a little simple painting, and glue some special touches in place to make an easy and adorable lamp. For this project, you need an electric drill fitted with a 3/8" bit.

MATERIALS

- Birdhouse/lighthouse lamp base (from Add Your Touch, see Sources)
- Fine grit sandpaper
- Wood filler
- Tack cloth
- Acrylic paints: white, black, red
- Four yellow cabochons
- Two mushroom birds
- Reindeer or Spanish moss
- Hot glue gun
- 25mm wood bead
- Pressure-sensitive felt
- 5" lamp pipe
- Side exit socket
- Cord set
- Harp wings
- Harp

INSTRUCTIONS

❶ Using a 3/8" bit, drill a hole about 1" deep in the very center top of the lighthouse.

❷ Using a nail set, tap in the nails joining the birdhouse together in the wood. Apply wood filler over the nail heads. Allow to dry. Sand the entire lamp base. Clean with a tack rag.

❸ Paint the entire lamp with white acrylic paint. Allow to dry. Apply another coat. Let dry. Paint the wood bead with two coats as well.

❹ Cut the felt to fit the bottom of the lamp. Remove the paper backing and press in place.

❺ Apply black paint to the square, flat top of the lighthouse and the four sloped roofs of the lighthouse top. Set aside to dry. Glue the lighthouse top on place.

❻ With a pencil, mark the lines for the lighthouse stripes as illustrated. Put masking tape along the lines, outside of where you want to paint the red stripe and paint it. Before the red paint dries, rub some off with a paper towel to give an aged look. Remove the masking tape. Repeat to complete the stripes.

❼ Using hot glue, attach the cabochons over the holes to simulate lights at the top of the lighthouse.

❽ Hot glue the moss along the edge of the base. Hot glue the bird to the perch.

❾ Wire the lamp as instructed on page 12.

❿ After installing the shade, screw the wooden bead to the top of the harp (drill the hole larger if necessary) and hot glue the second bird to the top of the bead, covering the hole.

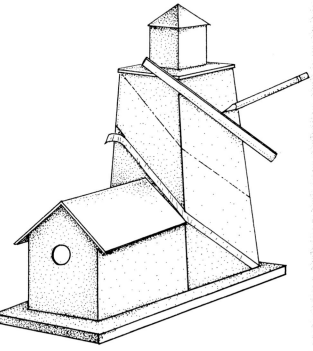

Torn Tissue Paper Sailboat Shade

Much like finger painting with glue and tissue, this technique is child's play, and so much fun I didn't want to stop. Honestly, it requires no skill.

You will find tissue paper at your local craft store, or turn to Dick Blick in the Sources section at the back of the book. Mod Podge is a matte finish, water-based sealer much like a glue, used for decoupage. It is widely available at craft stores and through most mail order suppliers of crafts and art materials.

MATERIALS

- 10" round washer top fitter ring
- 16" round fitter ring
- Pressure-sensitive styrene (see Sources)
- Sky blue acrylic or watercolor paint
- White tissue paper
- Three shades of blue/green tissue paper for water
- Yellow and blue/green tissue paper for boats
- Black or brown tissue paper for birds
- Scraps of white handmade paper or tissue paper for clouds
- Mod Podge
- Glue

Find the pattern for this lampshade on page 111.

INSTRUCTIONS

1 Cut the shade from the styrene. Lay the styrene down, sticky-side-up. Apply white tissue paper to the shade, using as many pieces as it takes to cover the entire surface. Don't worry about it being flat. In fact, the creases and folds in the tissue will make the finished shade more interesting. Trim where the tissue paper overlaps. In step 4 you can use some Mod Podge to glue the paper together where it overlaps. Trim the tissue paper around the outside edges.

2 Water down some blue acrylic paint and test on scraps until it is a light sky color. Paint as a wash on the tissue paper on the shade. Allow to dry.

3 Tear the "water"-colored tissue papers into approximately 1" to 1½" pieces. Apply Mod Podge to the bottom 3" of the shade. Lay the colored tissue pieces randomly on the Mod Podge, touching or not. Using a brush or sponge brush, apply more Mod Podge over the colored tissue paper, allowing the color to bleed onto the white tissue paper. Add more pieces randomly over, beside, and overlapping the first ones. Mod Podge the paper pieces in place. When you are pleased with the effect, set aside to dry.

4 Tear the tissue paper into boat and sail shapes. Mod Podge them in place, following the photos for guidance. Be sparing when brushing on the Mod Podge, as you don't want the colors to bleed too much. Do the same for the clouds and birds. Set aside to dry.

5 Following the instructions on page 20, glue the back seam of the shade and install the fitter rings.

6 Measure and mark lightly 3/4" down from the top and up from the bottom of the shade. Holding a metal yardstick down on the tissue paper, tear blue tissue paper into 1½"-wide strips. Mod Podge one strip to the top of the shade, just covering the marked line. Fold the remaining 3/4" of the strip to the back and glue in place. Using a paper towel, clean up most of the bleeding color dripping down the shade. Do the same for the bottom part of the shade.

7 Apply a coat of Mod Podge to the entire shade. Set aside

Silver Teapot Lamp

This charming lamp is easy to make with the help of a Dremel tool. I purchased my teapot at an antique mall for $25. It was in dire need of a polishing, which revealed the beauty underneath. To create a hole at the center top of the lid, I removed the little handle finial with a Dremel tool. Cut it like butter! Then I drilled through what was left with an electric drill. I found it easiest to do this from inside the lid.

To find the correct bolt and nut sizes in step 2, I took my teapot, socket, harp wings and lamp neck or coupling to the hardware store (after creating the hole in step 1). I put it together right there, took it home, and tightened it up. Done!

MATERIALS

- Teapot
- Nut, washer, and bolt
- Lamp neck or coupling
- Silver spray paint
- Side exit socket
- Harp wings
- Harp

INSTRUCTIONS

1 Using the Dremel tool, remove the finial handle from the teapot lid. Once removed, drill a hole in the center top of the lid.

2 Place the washer on the bolt from inside the lid, insert the bolt into the hole in the lid and push out through the top. Put the lamp neck and then the harp wings on the bolt. Push the bolt into the bottom of the socket. Screw the little nut on the bolt so the nut rests inside the bottom of the socket housing. Note: The screw shouldn't protrude above the neck.

3 Wire the lamp as instructed on page 12.

4 For the finial, I hot-glued the finial/handle I had removed from the top of the teapot to a 25mm wood ball bead. Then I covered the bead with dried flowers to match my lampshade. If you have trouble screwing the bead on the harp end, drill the hole a little bigger.

Dried Flower Shade

*T*he perfect accompaniment to the silver teapot lamp, this shade requires a lot of gluing—and a space where making a mess isn't a problem.

The ribbon used to trim the top of the lamp can be a little more or less than the 2¼" width called for. If this is the case, adjust the placement line you mark by the difference. To avoid drying out the flowers, be sure to use a 40 watt or lower bulb.

MATERIALS

- Muslin-covered styrene
- 7" round washer top fitter ring
- 10" round fitter ring
- Binding tape
- 2¼"-wide ribbon
- Bunch of blue delphinium
- Bunch of pink delphinium
- Bunch of celosia
- Sheet moss
- Glue
- Hot glue gun

Find the pattern for this lampshade on page 118.

INSTRUCTIONS

1 As instructed on pages 20 and 23, cut out the styrene, glue the back seam, install the top and bottom wires, and trim with twill tape.

2 Draw a line 1¾" below the top edge of the shade. Glue the ribbon to the top edge of the shade, having the bottom edge of the ribbon just cover the line. Turn the top edge of the ribbon to the back of the shade and glue it in place.

3 Cut or tear the sheet moss to make a manageable piece to cover about a 1/6 section of the shade and long enough to go top to bottom. Apply hot glue to the shade where the moss will go. Press the moss on the shade. Continue around the shade. Don't worry about neatness or matching the sections of moss along their vertical edges. You will trim and glue again later.

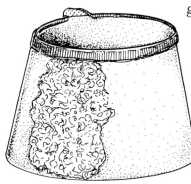

4 Tear the moss where the sections meet so they meld together. Pull the moss back slightly and apply hot glue. Trim and neaten up the top edge of the moss so it is neat along the ribbon.

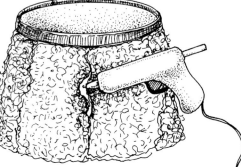

Sneak hot glue in underneath the moss as necessary.

5 Trim the moss along the bottom of the shade, even with the top edge of the binding.

6 Cut the celosia into pieces to unfold it. Glue to the bottom edge of the shade as shown.

7 Cut delphinium florets and glue them in a line above the celosia, alternating pink and blue. Do the same along the top edge of the moss, overlapping the bottom edge of the ribbon.

Yellow Plaid Painted Lamp with Decoupage Flowers

Talk about turning an ugly duckling into a swan! Both this and the next lamp were originally purchased at a superstore. Not exactly designer showroom fare. I bought them at a thrift shop for $3 or $4 a piece. One was a dark mauve, the other dark boring blue. They were in perfect shape electrically, so I removed the socket, felt bottom, and cord before working my makeover magic and simply replaced everything afterwards.

For both of these lamps, you will need only sandpaper and a screwdriver in the way of tools and a tack cloth to clean after sanding.

The lovely yellow lamp combines super simple painting and decoupage. First, I base coated the lamp then drew in lines and painted them—first vertically, then horizontally—to form plaid. Then I glued down flowers cut from wrapping paper. A few coats of varnish, and voila—a lovely little lamp!

Use a small pair of very sharp scissors to cut the flowers for the decoupage. Alternatively, you may wish to use a craft knife on a piece of glass or self-healing mat.

After painting and decoupaging, the lamp was very bright. The antiquing helped tone this down.

MATERIALS

- Ceramic thrift store lamp
- Delta Ceramcoat paints: Oyster White #2492, Opaque Yellow #2509
- Brushes: #12 shader, #8 shader, #6/0 liner, varnish brush
- Floral wrapping paper (to cut out the decoupage shapes)
- Mod Podge
- Warm Brown antiquing gel by Delta
- Water base matte varnish
- Pressure-sensitive felt

INSTRUCTIONS

1 Remove the felt from the bottom of the lamp. Pull the socket out of the socket cap and undo the wires. Pull the cord out of the hole in the side of the lamp. Reach inside the lamp and remove the lock washer and washer from the socket nipple. Remove the socket. Set these parts aside.

2 Sand the lamp to roughen it so the new paint will adhere. Clean with a tack cloth.

3 Base coat the lamp with two coats of Oyster White. If the lamp is a very dark color to start with, you may need three coats to cover. Allow to dry.

4 My lamp base is 6½" high. I marked the placement lines for the stripes by making four wide vertical stripes, spacing them evenly apart. I then added the horizontal stripes. Depending on the shape and size of your lamp base, you may wish to have more or fewer stripes and place the horizontal stripes higher or lower. You may be precise, as I was, by carefully measuring and marking the edges of the stripes. Or, for less fuss, make general markings and draw squiggly stripes.

5 For the wide vertical stripes, use the #12 shader brush. Next, use the #8 for the wide horizontal stripes. Last, use the 6/0 liner brush for the small horizontal stripes. For the top yellow section, paint the bottom edge neatly with a shader brush, then fill in to the top. Set aside to dry.

6 Carefully cut the flowers from the wrapping paper. Rather than leave background color showing, err on cutting into the flower. One at a time, apply Mod Podge to the back of the pieces and carefully press them in place, making sure the edges are securely glued and there are no bubbles underneath.

7 Once dry, paint on the antiquing gel. It will be very dark. Immediately after covering the entire lamp base with the gel, use a soft rag to gently remove the gel. Don't worry about removing too much; you can add more. Let dry.

8 Follow the manufacturer's instructions to apply multiple coats of varnish. I applied more than ten coats, making the edges of the cutouts disappear into the varnish so they don't appear to stand off the lamp. You can allow as little as ten minutes between coats, so it isn't as time-consuming as it sounds.

9 Reinstall the socket and cord.

10 Apply the pressure-sensitive felt to the bottom of the lamp.

Antique Hanky Shade

O n a trip to one of my favorite treasure haunts, I found two lovely hankies which said "lampshade" to me. They had a nice scalloped border completely around them and a dainty appliqué in one corner. I made use of nearly every bit of them to make this lamp.

MATERIALS

- *5" x 6" x 8" hexagon clip top shade frame (see Mainely Shades in Sources)*
- *Hug Snug (see Sources)*
- *White thread*
- *Two hankies, measuring approximately 14" square*
- *White bias tape binding*

INSTRUCTIONS

1 Wrap the frame with Hug Snug as instructed on page 21.

2 Cut the hankies as shown.

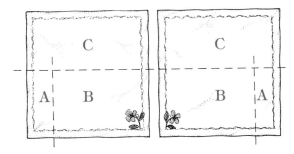

3 Match the long borders of pieces A and slipstitch them together from the wrong side along the butted border edges.

4 Center pieces A on one section of the frame, right-side-out. Fold pieces A over the top edge of the frame, having the bottom edges cover the bottom wire plus about 1/4". Stitch with a running stitch.

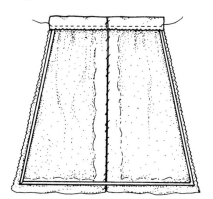

viewed from inside the frame

5 Clothespin the two hanky pieces B to the frame, all the way around the top. Let about 1/4" of the hanky extend below the bottom wire. Mark the center back. Right sides facing, mark and stitch a vertical line for the back seam. Trim away the extra fabric in the seam allowance.

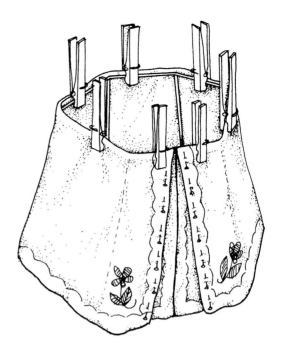

6 Using clothespins, arrange the two hanky pieces B on the front of the frame as shown. Clothespin to the frame at the top. Straight pin pieces B to pieces A. Whipstitch the two layers together in the border of pieces B, making sure the stitches don't show through on the right side. Trim the raw edges of pieces A to stitching.

7 Repin pieces B to the frame, attaching them with clothespins and folding the top raw edge over the top to the back. Let the bottom border edge extend about 1/4" below the bottom wire. Arrange the fabric evenly over the top edge, slightly gathering it as necessary. Using a running stitch, stitch the two layers together.

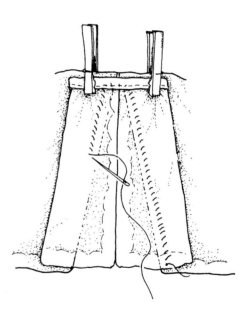

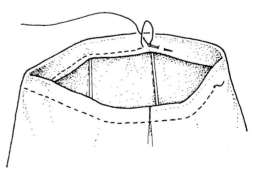

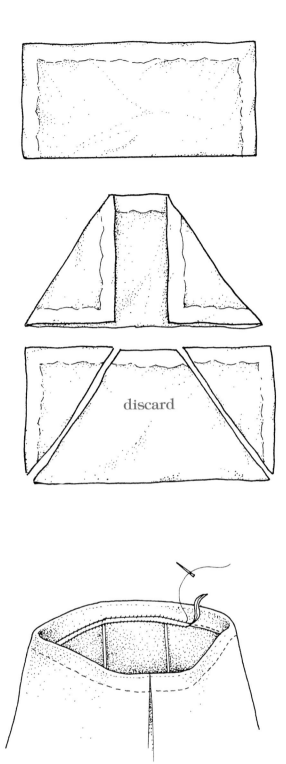

8 Fold and trim the four corner pieces C as shown. Center one at the front section of the frame, having the point extend about 2½" down. Pin in place. Do the same for a piece at the back. Repeat for the two sides. Attach them to the other pieces using a whipstitch, making sure not to stitch through the front. Remove excess fabric.

9 Trim the extra fabric from the seam allowances at the top of the frame. Stitch bias tape over the raw edges and stitching to hide.

discard

Floral Painted Lamp

So you think you can't paint? Believe me, you can. The key is using the right brush . If you are still not convinced, you can base coat the lamp and paint the strips, but eliminate painting the flowers by substituting decoupaged flowers strewn about.

My instructions for placement of the dividing lines between the blue and green sections of paint are based on the lamp base I used. Your lamp will most likely differ. Use your judgment when deciding where to place the lines.

MATERIALS

- Ceramic thrift store lamp
- Delta Ceramcoat paints: Silver Pine #2534, Liberty Blue #2416, Paynes Grey #2512, Light Ivory #2401
- Brushes: #12 shader, #8 shader, #6/0 liner, #5 round, varnish brush
- Water base satin varnish
- Pressure-sensitive felt

INSTRUCTIONS

1 Remove the felt from the bottom of the lamp. Pull the socket out of the socket cap and undo the wires. Pull the cord out of the hole in the side of the lamp. Reach inside the lamp and remove the lock washer and washer from the socket nipple. Remove the socket. Set these parts aside.

2 Sand the lamp to roughen it so the new paint will adhere. Clean with a tack cloth.

3 Base coat the lamp with two coats of Liberty Blue. If the lamp was a very dark color to start with, you may need three coats to cover. Allow to dry.

4 Mark lines at the top and bottom sections of the lamp to delineate the three paint areas: blue, green, blue. Paint the center section Silver Pine green.

5 Once dry, paint the flowers on the lamp base with the #5 round brush and Light Ivory paint, overlapping the color sections in a random pattern.

6 Add "leaves" interspersed among the flowers. Using the tip of the liner brush, dot the centers of the flowers with three dots of Liberty Blue.

7 Once dry, paint a Paynes Grey stripe over the top line, measuring a little over 1/8" wide. At the bottom line, paint a line a bit wider (mine is approximately 1/4" wide). Repeat at the bottom on the lamp. Using Light Ivory paint and the liner brush, make small angled dashes over the Paynes Grey.

8 Follow the manufacturer's instructions to apply three coats of varnish.

9 Reinstall the socket and cord.

10 Apply the pressure-sensitive felt to the bottom of the lamp.

*L*ace-Stenciled Wooden Lampshade

*Y*es, this is a solid wood shade, not veneer. It's built in four pieces and comes ready to finish. And it's American-made in Kansas!

The lace fabric I used as a stencil for spray painting is a widely available curtain fabric. I lined up my pattern for each section of the shade along the lace edge as best I could. I found in the end I needn't have fretted so much about how the pattern would look when fin-ished. It is so soft a look that it didn't matter that the pattern did-n't match.

I used white spray paint and expected to want to tone down the color with an antiquing wash. Not so. The effect from stenciling through the fabric is so subtle that the white wasn't glaring.

The creator of the wooden shade recommends using a bulb intended for a fan.

MATERIALS

- Wooden shade #41007CF4 (see The Elbridge Co. in Sources)
- Lace fabric
- Wood stain
- Spray mount
- White or ivory spray paint
- Gold paint (I used Accent Crown Jewels #2527 Kings Gold)
- Varnish

INSTRUCTIONS

1 Stain the shade. Set aside to dry.

2 Make paper patterns of the four sections of the lampshade. Use these to cut four pieces of lace fabric.

3 Apply spray mount to the back of the lace pieces. Press to the shade. Set atop a can and spray paint with a light touch. Be careful that the blast from the can doesn't blow the edges of the lace. Let dry.

4 Paint the inside of the shade with two coats of gold paint.

5 Apply three coats of varnish, sanding lightly between coats. Let dry.

Strawberry Jar Lamp

Create a perennial flower display with this strawberry jar lamp full of painted metal flowers. The painting is easy—just a little layering and blending.

When cutting the foil, protect your hands by wearing a pair of leather gloves.

Visit the bridal section of your local fabric/crafts store to find the centers for the red and blue flowers.

You will need an electric drill and 3/8" and 1/4" bits for this project.

MATERIALS

- 7"-8" tall strawberry jar
- 6" diameter saucer
- Styrofoam
- 9" lamp pipe
- 1½" threaded nipple (available from lamp suppliers)
- Coupler (available from lamp suppliers)
- Small washer
- Large washer
- Bottom exit socket
- Cord set
- Moss
- Brass tooling foil (see Dick Blick in Sources)
- Delta Perm Enamel paints: Metal Primer, Clear Gloss, Ultra Black, Red Red, Ultra White, Emperor Blue, Light Blue, Citrus Yellow, Tangerine, True Green, Apple Candy Green
- Bunched flower centers
- Individual flower stamens
- 18-gauge covered floral wire
- 16-gauge floral wire
- Floral tape
- Three 3/4" buttons
- Black dimensional paint
- Moss
- Black 1/4" bugle beads
- Pressure-sensitive felt

Find the patterns for this lamp on page 121.

INSTRUCTIONS

Each of the six yellow flowers is made of three petal pieces. The three red flowers are made of two flower pieces each. The centers are buttons. Each of the six blue flowers consists of one flower piece. I made 18 leaves—nine for the top section and three for each of the three pockets.

❶ Trace the patterns from page 121. Glue them to lightweight cardboard and cut them out. Trace them onto the tooling foil. It will be easier to cut if you first cut it into strips a bit wider than the flower you're working on.

❷ Place a ruler lengthwise over a leaf piece. Fold the leaf along the straight edge of the ruler. Repeat for each of the leaves.

❸ Following the manufacturer's instructions, apply metal primer to the pieces. Using the color designated on the pattern pieces, base coat the fronts, let dry, then base coat the backs of the pieces. Apply another coat to the backs.

❹ **Yellow flowers**: Base coat with Citrus Yellow. Apply Tangerine to the tips and ultra white to the center. Using Citrus Yellow, blend the colors.

Red flowers: Base coat with Red Red. Apply a little strip of Ultra White to the center of each petal. Using Red Red, cover the petals with red, blending in the white to barely show. Apply Ultra Black in short strokes at the center of three of the flowers, starting the strokes toward the outside and pulling in. These will be the fronts of the finished flowers.

Blue flowers: Base coat with Emperor Blue. Drizzle Ultra White paint on your palette. Drop some Emperor Blue and Light Blue on top. Dip your brush in and paint onto a petal so the color is streaked. Do this for both sides of the flower pieces.

Leaves: Base coat with True Green. Apply Citrus Yellow in a line along the center of the leaf. (I did four or five leaves at a time, then wiped my brush.) Apply Apple Candy Green to the outside edges of the leaves, then blend the two colors.

❺ Glaze as directed on the label.

❻ Finish the yellow flowers by trimming the beads from the two ends of five stamen pieces. Dip the ends in glue and insert them into bugle beads. Allow to dry. Using a nail, hammer a hole in the center of each petal. Do this on a block of wood. Push one half piece of 16-gauge wire through a flower piece from the back, then add two more flower pieces. Bend the wire and push the end back in the hole to the back. Insert the group of five stamens together through the resulting loop and center them. Pull the wire to the back, catching and securing the stamen wires at their centers. Wrap the wire around itself. Cut the covered wire into thirds. Wrap the thinner wire around one piece. Arrange the petals.

Wrap the wires with the floral tape. Bend the tips of the petals back slightly.

❼ Finish the red flowers by hammering a nail hole in the center of each flower piece. Do this on a block of wood. Put two flower pieces, one plain and one painted with black and white, on half a piece of 16-gauge wire. From the right side of the flowers, put a button on the

wire and turn the wire back on itself and push back through. Wrap the wire around itself. Wrap the thinner wire around 1/3 piece of the covered wire. Wrap the wires with the floral tape.

❽ Finish the blue flowers by hammering a nail hole in the center of each petal. Do this on a block of wood. Paint the balls of the flower centers black. I used clothespins to clamp their bent wire stems to a paper plate to dry. Push the flower center through a flower piece. Cut the covered wire into thirds. Wrap the thinner wire around one piece. Bend the flower as shown. Wrap the wires with floral tape.

❾ Finish the leaves by pinching the pointed end of the leaf. Apply glue and lay 1/3 of a piece of covered wire in the glue. Let dry thoroughly. Bend the wire and the other end of the leaf as shown.

CONSTRUCT THE LAMP

1 Turn the saucer upside-down. Center the strawberry jar over the saucer. From inside the pot, mark the pot's drainage hole on the saucer. Drill a 3/8" hole at the marking.

2 On the side edge of the saucer, drill a 1/4" hole for the cord to go through.

3 Cut a piece of Styrofoam 3/4" shorter than the pot. Trim one side so it just goes into the pot when pushed hard. Remove.

4 Turn the pot upside-down. Using the 3/8" bit, drill straight down through the drainage hole through the Styrofoam. Remove the Styrofoam.

5 Push the pipe through the hole in the Styrofoam. Put the coupler on one end of the 9" pipe so half the coupler is threaded on. Thread the nipple on the coupler snugly. Place a small and then large washer on the nipple. Insert the threaded nipple into the pot and poke out the bottom. Put the saucer in place, putting the end of the pipe through the hole. Screw on a washer first and then a nut. Tighten.

6 Turn the strawberry jar/saucer right-side-up. Cut pieces of Styrofoam and insert them into the pockets of the pot to bolster the large piece and to take up room in the holes where you will later insert the painted flower. Add the smaller pieces to make the Styrofoam firm in the pot.

7 Install the socket and cord set as instructed on page 12, having the cord go through the hole in the side of the saucer.

8 Hot glue moss over the Styrofoam at the top of the pot and in the holes.

9 Arrange the flowers and poke their stems into the Styrofoam.

10 Place the saucer over a piece of cardboard. Trace around it. Cut out inside the traced line. Apply felt. Glue to the bottom of the saucer.

Lace-Covered Umbrella Lampshade

*V*isit the home decorating department of your local fabric/craft store to find the lace window treatments I used on this shade. The base fabric is a poly/cotton blend, which I figured would have a little more stretch to go smoothly around the frame than a pure cotton. The crystal prisms offer an excellent excuse for a foray to an antique show. Here in Florida, a vendor at a monthly show sells all sorts of chandelier prisms. And home improvement stores carry new ones.

MATERIALS

- *Heather lampshade (see Mainely Shades in Sources)*
- *Hug Snug (see Sources)*
- *Lace fabric*
- *White fabric*
- *White thread*
- *Three yards flat trim*
- *Six chandelier prisms*

INSTRUCTIONS

1 Wrap the shade frame with Hug Snug as instructed on page 21.

2 Cut a piece of white base fabric larger than one section of the frame, including the bottom section. Lay the white fabric piece over one section of the frame. Whipstitch to the Hug Snug. Wrap fabric over the shade wire at the top and bottom and to the back. Trim the edges close to the stitching. Repeat for all sections.

4 Cut a piece of trim 2" longer than the length of a vertical spine. Stitch over the spine, covering the raw edges of the fabric and previous stitching and folding the raw end to the back. If the trim tends to fray, apply a seam sealer. Stitch trim around the top opening.

5 Hand stitch a prism to the bottom of each rib.

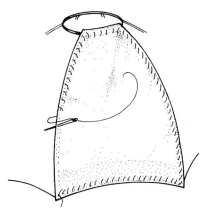

3 Similarly, stitch lace fabric over the base fabric. Repeat for all sections.

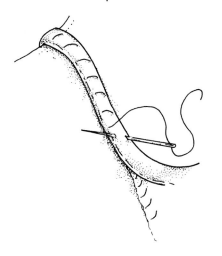

Bunny Doorstop Lamp

Searching for a cement garden bunny to turn into a lamp, I happened upon this adorable bunny on the Internet. Upon its arrival, it clearly called for a base, which had to be a box edged with pickets. Naturally.

To construct the box I bought two three foot long boards, one 1" x 2" and one 1/2" x 8". You may skip the sawing step if you wish by asking to have the wood cut at the store. Then all you will need is to do some drilling. You will need drill bits in three sizes: 5/32", 1/4", and 3/8".

MATERIALS

- Hopping Bunny Doorstop (see Aragon in Sources)
- Large package of jumbo craft sticks
- Two 13"-long pieces of 1" x 2" boards for the sides of the box
- Two 13¾"-wide pieces of 1/2" x 8" boards for the top and bottom
- Two 2"-long pieces of 1/2" x 8" boards for the ends
- 24 3/4"wood screws for making the base

- Two 1" wood screws for attaching the bunny to the base
- 4" lamp pipe
- Side exit socket
- Cord set
- Harp wings
- Harp
- Sheet moss
- Glue
- Hot glue gun
- White paint

INSTRUCTIONS

1 Drill holes with the 5/32" drill bit in both the top and bottom and both ends of the box. These will be pilot holes for the screws to hold the box together. Using a 1/4" drill bit, make "countersink" holes about 1/8" deep at each of the holes you drilled.

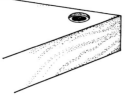

2 Drill holes in one of the top/bottom pieces as shown for the screws to go into the bottom of the bunny. This will be the top of the box. Center the bunny on the top piece of the box, on the side where you made the countersink holes, with the countersink holes up. Trace

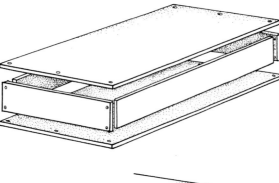

around the bunny. Do this over a sink so you can get a pencil from underneath through the holes in the wood to mark the bottom of the bunny. Drill holes at the markings in the bottom of the bunny with the 5/32" drill bit.

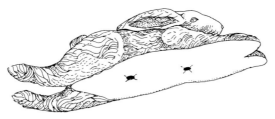

3 Use the 3/8" drill bit to drill a hole for the lamp pipe between the bunny's ears. Drill it about 3/4" deep, which will be enough to cover the threads of the lamp pipe when inserted.

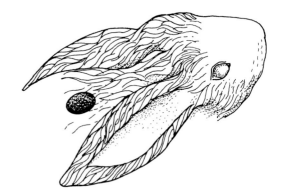

4 Screw the short box sides to the long box sides. Screw the bottom of the box, countersunk-hole-side-up, to the sides. Turn right-side-up.

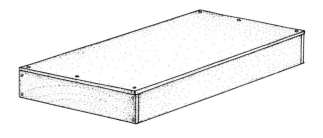

5 Hot glue moss to the top of the box top (the side with the countersink holes). Don't glue moss along the edges where the screw holes are or inside the marked lines. The object is to put down moss so the bunny will look like it is resting on top of the moss.

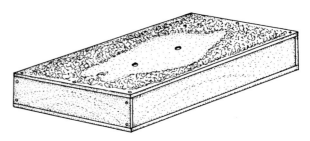

6 Place the bunny on the box top, following the outline. From underneath, screw the bunny in place. I did this over a sink, working up from inside the sink. Screw the top of the box to the top of the box sides.

7 Using scissors, trim one end of each craft stick as shown. Trim the other end of one square so it measures 5¼" in length. Use this one as a template to cut all the other craft sticks.

8 Paint the front and back of the craft sticks white.

9 Hot glue the craft sticks in place. For each side, first glue one at each end. Then work towards the center, placing the craft sticks side-by-side. If you find as you get close to filling the gap that you have a little extra room, leave a bit of space between the sticks.

10 Glue more moss to the box top to cover the box. Glue wisps of moss between craft stick pickets to cover spaces between pickets as necessary.

11 Glue the lamp pipe in the hole.

12 Install the harp and harp wings, socket, and cord.

Brass Chicken Wire Lampshade

A snap to make, this shade is simply styrene covered with hand-made paper, then wrapped with brass chicken wire. Easy!

The brass chicken wire is available from Constantine's (see Sources). I purchased 12", which left just enough scrap for comfort.

I have to admit, the green handmade paper I bought for my shade wasn't wide enough to accommodate the 38⅛" I needed for the shade, so I pieced a section in at the back of the shade. Due to the texture of the paper and the fact that the brass chicken wire covered it, it doesn't even show. I found the green paper at a local art store. You can find similar papers through Dick Blick (see Sources) or make your own.

MATERIALS

- 7" x 38⅛" pressure-sensitive styrene
- 9½" x 12" oval washer top ring (see *Mainely Shades* in Sources)
- 9½" x 12" oval bottom wire
- Handmade paper
- Glue
- 12" piece of brass chicken wire
- Wire cutters

Find the pattern for this lamp on page 122.

Find the pattern for this lamp on page 122.

INSTRUCTIONS

❶ Lay the styrene paper-side-up on your work surface. Apply the handmade paper. Trim the paper to 1/2" beyond the edge of the styrene all the way around. At the short edges, turn to the inside and glue. Glue the short edges together, overlapping 1/2".

❷ Clamp and weight as shown on page 20.

❸ Install the wire oval rings as instructed on page 20, placing the seam in the styrene at the center of one long edge of the oval. This will be the back.

❹ Using a cotton swab, apply glue to the inside edge of the paper at the top and bottom of the frame, turn to the inside, and press in place.

❺ Roll out the brass chicken wire so the cut edges are at the top and bottom. With wire cutters, trim the bottom edge so it is straight, trimming through the center of a horizontal row of "squares." Place the shade on top. Adjust the shade so it is about 1" above the cut edge. Cut the top edge about 1" above the shade, again, through the center of a horizontal row of "squares."

❻ Starting with one short finished edge at the seam, center the chicken wire over the styrene. Turn the top and bottom edges of the chicken wire neatly and crisply to the inside of the shade. Work your way all the way around the shade. Go back around, turning the raw edges under.

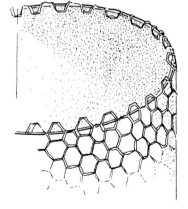

Victorian Gingerbread Lamp

Do you recognize these as the beautiful brackets decorating the porches of Victorian homes? Turn the book upside-down. Now you see!

I chose rather large brackets to make a grand lamp. Victorian Millworks offers many other bracket designs and you may find a few choices at your local home center as well.

For this project, you will need an electric drill with 3/8" and 9/64" drill bits.

I found the large wooden finial at a craft store.

MATERIALS

- Four Victorian gingerbread brackets (#414-L from Anthony Wood Products)
- 1" x 1½"-wide piece of wood
- Eight wood dowel pins
- Wood glue
- Eight 2"-wide wooden toy wheels (see Cherry Tree Toys in Sources)
- Eight 1" wood screws
- Delta acrylic paints: White, Sea Green

- Aleene's Crackle Medium 1 and 2
- 7" lamp pipe
- Two lamp nuts
- Bottom exit socket
- Cord set
- Harp
- Harp wings
- Large wooden finial
- Threaded finial adapter

INSTRUCTIONS

❶ Cut the wood into four 1¾"-long pieces. These will be the spacers to hold the brackets together.

❷ Drill a 3/8" hole in the center of one wood piece for the lamp pipe. This will be the top spacer piece.

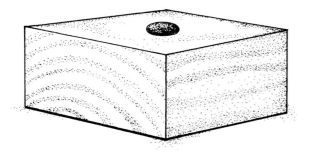

❸ Drill 3/8" holes into the opposing sides of each of the four 1½" spacer pieces. Set two aside.

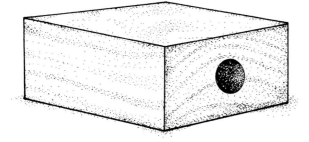

❹ Insert dowel pins into one side hole in each of two spacers. One of them should be the one drilled for the lamp pipe. Use it first, so it will be the top-most spacer in the lamp.

❺ Mark the long back edges of two brackets as shown. This will be an opposing pair of brackets on the finished lamp.

2"

3"

6 Match the top edge of the spacer that has the hole for the lamp pipe to the marked line. Mark on the bracket where the dowel pin hits the bracket. Drill a 3/8" hole at the marking. Repeat for the other spacer. Insert the dowel pins into the holes you just drilled in the bracket.

7 Insert dowel pins into the other two holes in the spacers. On a level surface, match up the second bracket of the pair to the first, back-to-back with the spacers in between and mark the second bracket where the dowels hit. Drill 3/8" holes at the markings. Insert the dowel pins to check placement.

9 Detach the last bracket and re-setup the pair to lock with the first pair. Make sure everything fits squarely. Take one set apart. Glue the dowel pins in. Take the other set apart. Glue around the first set. Before taking them apart, you may wish to mark a key so you know that dowel pin one goes to hole one on a bracket, etc.

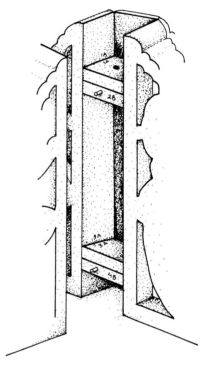

10 On the non-flat side of the wheels, drill countersink holes with the 3/8" drill bit.

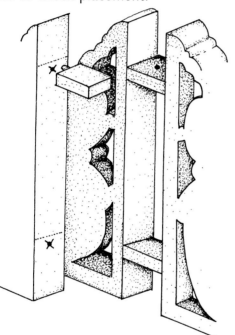

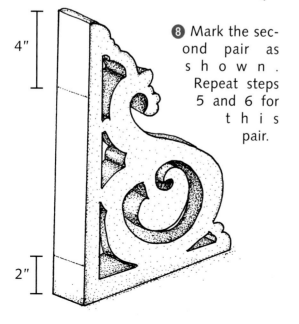

8 Mark the second pair as shown. Repeat steps 5 and 6 for this pair.

4"

2"

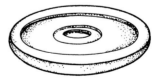

11 Mark the bottom of each bracket with a dot 7/8" in from each end and centered. Drill pilot holes for the feet screws at the dots. Screw the wheel "feet" to the bottoms of the brackets.

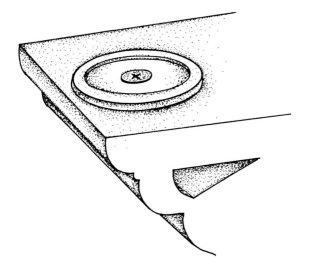

12 Paint the lamp and finial with two coats of Sea Green paint.

13 Following the manufacturer's instructions, apply the first mosaic step.

14 Apply white paint.

15 Following the manufacturer's instructions, apply the second mosaic step.

16 Put a nut on the lamp pipe. Insert this end into the hole in the top spacer. Glue in place if you wish.

17 Install the other nut, harp, socket, and cord as instructed on page 12.

18 To prepare the finial to attach it to the lamp, glue a finial adapter to the bottom of the finial. Since my finial had a cutout bottom, I cut a double layer of cork in circles to fit the opening. I then drilled a hole in the cork the size of the adapter and glued the adapter in place.

Wisteria Sponge-Stamped Lampshade

*S*tamp paint a lampshade with makeup sponges? Sure! It's free-form fun!

MATERIALS

Small Flair lampshade frame (see Mainely Shades in Sources)
1½ yards duck fabric
Delta Ceramcoat paints: Green Sea, Golden Brown, Ice Storm

Violet, Wisteria, White, Gesso
Makeup sponges
Glue
#4 round brush

Find the pattern for the valance on page 124.

INSTRUCTIONS

1 To make the lampshade pattern, roll the shade a section at a time on a large piece of paper, tracing above the top and below the bottom rings. Draw in lines at the sides at the last wire. Add 1/2" to one of these lines. Cut out the pattern.

2 Trace the valance pattern from page 124 and cut it out.

3 Using a yardstick, draw a diagonal line from one corner of the duck to the other. Make another line 1½" away. Cut out. This is the binding for the bottom of the shade.

④ Trace the shade and valance patterns on the duck. Cut out, leaving about 1" around the drawn lines.

⑤ Apply gesso to both the shade and valance fabric. Let dry.

⑥ Paint Sea Green on the other side of the valance piece. Let dry.

⑦ About 1/4" from the scalloped edge of the valance, paint a white line with a #4 round brush. Let dry. Just inside that line, paint another line, this time with Wisteria.

⑧ Trim one sponge into a long wispy leaf form. Use the entire length of the sponge. Trim another in a thin arching branch shape. For the flower stamp, trim the wide end of a third sponge into an approximately round shape. The shape doesn't matter too much as long as it doesn't have any square edges.

⑨ Lay and align the valance on the lampshade duck, which should be gesso-side-up. This way you will know where to sponge stamp the wisteria. Refer to the photo to sponge stamp the wisteria design. Dab the sponge in the paint, then blot on a paper towel before stamping. Create the structure of the vines using Golden Brown for the branches. Add the flowers using Wisteria, then use Sea Green for the leaves. Vary the way you hold the sponge as you dab. This way, your branches, flowers, and stems will have variety. To add a little dimension to the flowers, dab a little Ice Storm Violet over them. Allow to dry.

⑩ Place the painted duck on the shade frame, holding it at the top with clothespins. Overlap 1/2" at the back. Glue and press. Come back a few minutes later and make sure there is good contact between the two layers.

⑪ If necessary, trim the top and bottom edges of the duck shade even with the wire.

⑫ Draw a line on the back (gessoed) top edge of the valance, 1/2" below the top. Make perpendicular cuts every 1/2" or so.

⓭ Clothespin the valance to the top of the shade, keeping the drawn line even with the top wire/edge of the stamped shade. Place the overlap at the back where the shade seam is. Glue the back seam of the valance. Let dry.

⓮ Remove the clothespins. Turn the top edge of the valance to the back, covering the top wire of the shade. Clip as necessary to make the fabric fold back smoothly and to work around the shade ribs going to the center of the shade.

⓯ Draw a line 1/2" above the bottom edge of the shade. Apply glue below the line. Glue the duck strip even with the line. Let dry. Apply glue to the inside free edge of the duck strip. Press to the back. Let dry. Paint with gesso.

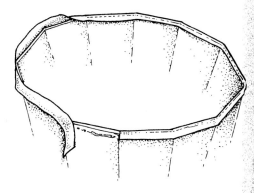

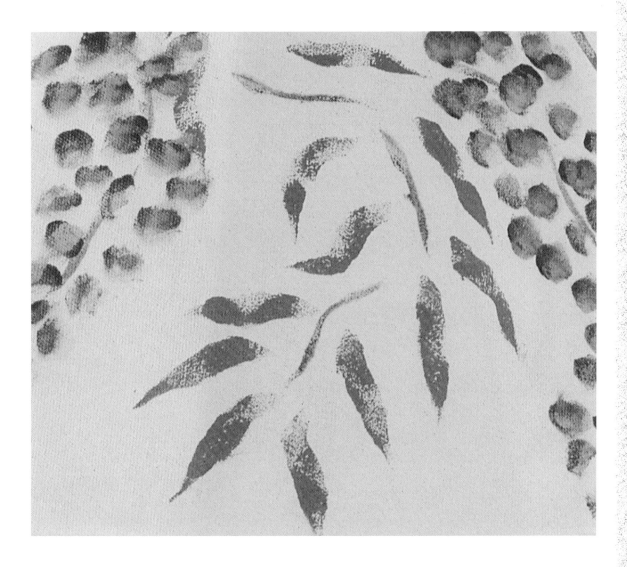

Basket Lamp

A nifty little adapter makes turning a basket into a lamp a snap. My basket has a flat handle so I drilled a hole in the handle and screwed a bolt from underneath into G & J Wholesales' basket adapter #02-160. Alternatively, choose a clamping adapter from any of the three lamp suppliers (see Sources).

Fill the basket with dried flowers as I have, or leave it empty so you can change the contents. Consider collectibles such as dolls or teddy bears, fruit, or skeins of yarn. The hydrangea can be ordered from Oak Ridge Farms (see Sources).

If the bottom of the basket isn't quite flat, screw four large wood beads to the bottom.

MATERIALS

- Basket
- Adapter (see above)
- Cord set
- Harp wings
- Harp
- Green Styrofoam oasis
- Hot glue gun
- Super glue
- Silk hydrangeas
- Kitchen knob for finial
- Finial adapter

INSTRUCTIONS

❶ Drill a hole in the basket handle. From underneath, insert the bolt through the hole. Put the harp wings on the bolt. Insert the bolt into the socket. Tighten.

❷ Glue the foam oasis to the inside bottom of the basket. Fill the basket with the hydrangea, trimming the stems as required.

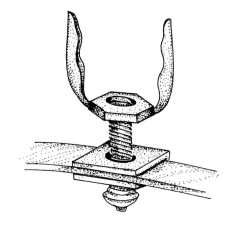

❸ Wire the socket as instructed on page 12.

❹ To make the finial, hacksaw the bolt off the knob. Use super glue to attach the finial adapter.

Plaid Painted Lampshade

While painting this shade I wondered why I didn't just use plaid fabric. But when finished, I installed a bulb and turned on the switch. Then I remembered. The quality of the light that comes through that antiqued translucent paper is fabulous.

Masa is a sturdy Japanese paper with a smooth, even texture which I chose for its translucency. If you can't find it locally in an art supply store, contact Jerry's Artarama listed in the Sources section.

I found the wonderful tasseled trim at a Calico Corners. Take your painted shade material in and they'll be happy to help you find a trim to match. Or start with one of their scrumptious trims to choose the colors to paint your plaid shade instead of those I used.

MATERIALS

- Addy shade frame (see Mainely Shades in Sources)
- Masa paper
- Delta Ceramcoat paints: Straw, Oyster White, Aquamarine, Napa Wine, Green Sea
- Brushes: #12 shader, #8 shader, #0 round
- Warm Brown antiquing gel by Delta

- Matte spray varnish
- Binding tape (see lamp suppliers in Sources)
- Two yards braid trim
- 1½ yards fringe trim
- Wire-edged ribbon
- Glue
- Super glue
- Kitchen knob for finial
- Finial adapter

PAINTING THE SHADE

1 On a very large piece of paper or newspaper, roll the shade section-by-section and trace around the outside of the wires to make a pattern. Start with a side rib, which is where the overlap will be. Don't include the bottom sections of the frame as these will be covered with the paper ribbon, not the painted Masa.

2 Cut out and trace the pattern onto the Masa. Base coat the Masa inside the marked pattern with Straw paint mixed with Oyster White in a 3:1 ratio. The colors will be toned down when antiqued. Let the paint dry.

3 Using Straw paint and the #12 shader, make vertical stripes about 2" apart and perpendicular to the top and bottom edges of the frame. Let dry.

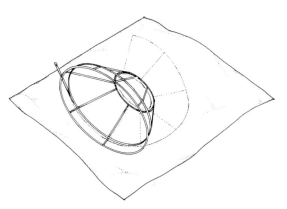

4 With the #8 shader, make Oyster White stripes next to the Straw stripes you just made. Let dry.

5 Starting about 1" from the top marking, use the #12 shader to make a vertical Green Sea stripe, following the shape of the frame. Repeat with two more Green Sea stripes, spaced about 1½" apart. Let dry.

6 Using the round brush, make stripes with Aquamarine paint to the right of the Oyster White stripes. Let dry.

7 To make them look as though they are atop the green stripes, redo the Oyster White stripes where they go over the green stripes. Let dry.

8 With the round brush, make Napa Wine stripes about 1/4" below the Green Sea stripes. Let dry.

9 Spray with two coats of varnish, allowing it to dry between coats.

10 Apply the antiquing gel. Wipe off with a paper towel. If the effect is too light, apply again.

11 Cut out the shade about 1/2" outside of the marked lines. On one side edge, trim to the marked line.

CONSTRUCTING THE SHADE

1 Cut the paper ribbon into 4"-long pieces. Center and bend the paper ribbon over the bottom two horizontal wires of the shade as shown. Apply glue to one raw edge of the ribbon. Press in place and clamp with a clothespin. In the same way, glue another paper ribbon piece, overlapping the first. Apply a little glue at the back of the first piece along the edge where the second piece will overlap. When you reach a vertical rib, make a cut in the top of the ribbon.

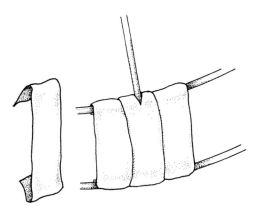

2 Using clothespins, fit the shade to the frame. Remove. Apply glue to the top ring of the shade. Clamp the shade paper in place. Glue the overlap at the side. Let dry.

3 Apply glue to the paper ribbon on the topmost of the two bottom rings. Press the bottom of the shade in place. Let dry. (Clamps aren't long enough to reach, so come back after five minutes and again after ten minutes to press again. With one hand inside the shade and one outside, press the shade paper to ensure good contact with the paper ribbon.)

4 Trim the excess Masa at the top and bottom.

5 As instructed on page 23, glue binding tape to the top edge of the frame, enclosing the top edge of the Masa and the top wire of the frame. Look at the width of the trim to judge how much of the bias to allow on the front side. Make cuts in the binding as necessary to get around the radial arm wires inside the lamp.

6 Glue braid trim to the top edge of the shade, covering the bias.

7 Glue braid trim to the bottom edge of the Masa directly over the horizontal wire. I applied glue all the way around, then held one hand inside to feel the wire while pressing the braid in place. This made it easier to center. You may want to use a seam sealer such as Fray Check to prevent the cut ends of the trim from raveling.

8 Apply glue to the paper ribbon below the bottom trim. Press the fringe trim in place.

9 For the finial, hacksaw the bolt from the end of the knob. Super glue a finial adapter in its place.

Stacked Cheese Box Lamp

Farm, village, and harbor—paint these bucolic scenes on three cheese boxes and turn them into a charming lamp. Don't be afraid of the painting. It's a simple matter of layering simple shapes on swaths of color.

Your nearby home center will cut the square for the lamp base. I purchased a 1" (which is really 3/4") x 8" piece of board in the shortest length available, which happened to be two feet. They made two cuts to create the square I needed.

For painting the boxes, use good-quality brushes. For the buildings, you'll find a #12 shader helpful. For the details, choose a small round brush, like a #0, or a liner.

To complete the project you need an electric drill and a 3/8" drill bit.

MATERIALS

- Three stacking boxes: 5", 6", and 6½" diameter
- Fruitwood Staining Gel by Delta
- Delta Ceramcoat acrylic paints: Black, White, Aquamarine #02498, Ocean Reef Blue #02074, Opaque Red #02507, Barn Red #02490, Seminole Green #02009, Charcoal #02436, Opaque Yellow #02509, Green Isle #02008, Green Sea #02445, Burnt Sienna #02030, Hunter Green #02471, Wisteria #02467
- Black permanent ink pen
- Spray sealer
- 4" lamp pipe
- 7" lamp pipe
- Coupler
- Two washers
- Two nuts
- Side exit socket
- Lamp cord set
- Harp wings
- Harp
- 6¾" square wood base
- Four 1" toy wheels
- Four 3/4" wood screws
- Styrofoam
- Pressure-sensitive felt

INSTRUCTIONS

1 Using a sponge brush, stain the box bottoms with the staining gel.

2 Paint the box tops, wheels, and base with two coats of Charcoal, allowing the paint to dry between coats.

3 Paint the boxes in layers as follows. I move back and forth between features to allow a little drying time. My instructions follow my process.

Top box: Mix Aquamarine with White and paint in an irregular 5"-wide swath for the sky. Don't worry about the bottom edge. You can paint the water over the sky. For clouds, dab on White mixed with a little Blue. Using Ocean Reef Blue, paint the water, making a straight horizontal line across the sky for the horizon. Mix with a little White and paint on top in soft patches. Paint a square-topped White cone for the lighthouse. Paint in three melon slices boats. Use Barn Red and/or Seminole Green. Paint Red stripes on the lighthouse. Paint Yellow for the light above the White of the lighthouse. Paint Charcoal masts for the boats. Mix a little White with Charcoal and dab around for rocks under the lighthouse. Make some darker and some lighter rocks. Paint in the sails with White. Paint the gulls and the dark details at the top and bottom of the lighthouse with Charcoal. Add wisps of straight Ocean Reef Blue and White to the water around the lighthouse and boats.

Middle box: Paint a 5½" swath of Seminole Green for the grass. Paint the church White. Don't worry about the edges that the roof will cover. Paint a Burnt Sienna square for the store. Paint two adjoining Opaque Yellow squares for the house, one smaller than the other. Paint the store's front door Yellow. Mix some White with Charcoal and paint the store roof. Paint the church and house roofs with Black, as well as the church's front door and the windows on the two buildings. Paint a Black shutter on each side of the store's front door. Paint the house front door Ocean Reef Blue. With Barn Red, paint two chimneys on the house and a chimney for the store. With the tip of the brush, paint the trees in dots with Hunter Green and add dots of Green Isle. With Burnt Sienna, paint trunks for the trees. With Charcoal and White, make faint wisps of smoke coming from the chimneys. Add Opaque Red dots with the very tip of the brush for apples. Paint the fence White. First paint the posts about 1/4" apart, then add the pickets and faintly paint in horizontal members, using a very light touch. Draw in lines at the windows with a black permanent ink pen to make window panes.

Bottom box: Paint the grass Seminole Green, about 6" wide. Make the shape irregular to suggest hills. Dab on some Green Isle. You may wish to use a paper towel, sponge, or your finger. Lighten Barn Red with a little Opaque Red and paint the barn shape. Paint the White house. Mix White into Charcoal and make stone walls from roundish dots to suggest rocks. Go over them with darker and lighter shades of the mix. Paint the barn roof with this mix. Paint the house windows with Opaque Yellow and the house roof and shutters with Charcoal. Make the trees and bushes with dots of Hunter Green. Paint tree trunks and the house chimney with Burnt Sienna. Paint the house front door with Barn Red. Paint the barn detail White. Dot Opaque Red apples on the trees. Make tiny dots with Wisteria on the bushes near the house to suggest lilacs. Add White/Charcoal wisps of smoke coming from the chimney. Make tiny Opaque Yellow dots in the barnyard for dandelions. Draw in lines at the windows with a black permanent ink pen to suggest window panes.

4 Spray all painted parts with sealer, following the manufacturer's instructions.

5 Using the 3/8" drill bit, drill the tops of the holes in the non-smooth sides of the four wheels bigger so you can countersink the screws even with the wheels. With a 5/32" bit, make starter holes 5/8" in from the corners of the bottom of the base. Screw feet on the base. Cut a round piece of felt for each of the four wheel feet. Peel off the paper backing and apply.

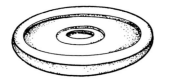

6 Cut Styrofoam to fit inside each of the boxes. Fill in with smaller pieces. This will give the boxes added support.

7 Put the tops on the boxes. Trace each box top on paper and cut out. Fold the paper in half twice to find the centers. Make holes at the centers, place on the box tops, and mark through the holes with chalk. Drill 3/8" holes through the top, down through the Styrofoam and through the bottom of each box.

8 Remove the box top and Styrofoam of the medium box. Screw the 4" piece of lamp pipe into the coupler so it takes up about half the length of the coupler. Insert the end without the coupler through the medium box from inside the box. Insert it in the top of the largest box and out the bottom. Insert from the top of the base through the hole out the bottom. Put a washer and then a nut on the pipe and secure.

9 Screw the 7" pipe into the coupler.

Put the Styrofoam, then the lid to the medium box on. Then the smallest box. Put a nut on the pipe, then the harp wings. Wire the lamp as instructed on page 12.

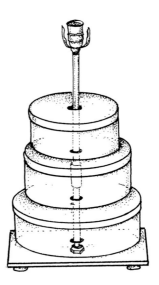

Embossed Wallpaper Shade

What a discovery. Embossed wallpaper is fun! Though the lampshade shown here was only stained, I did experiment with painting some of the raised designs as well. It didn't work for this lampshade, but is a great idea to keep in mind.

I found the embossed wallpaper at a national home supply store. I chose a small pattern to keep the shade in scale with my lamp. You can also order from books of embossed wallpaper patterns.

MATERIALS

- Embossed wallpaper
- 5" round washer top fitter ring
- 10" round bottom fitter ring
- Pressure-sensitive styrene
- Stain
- Spray varnish
- Glue
- Binding tape
- 3/8" grosgrain ribbon
- 5/8" grosgrain ribbon

Find the pattern for this lampshade on page 125.

INSTRUCTIONS

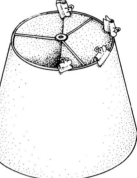

1 Stain a piece of wallpaper generously large enough for the pattern. Let dry.

2 Lay the styrene paper-side-up on a clean work surface. Place the lampshade pattern on the top. Weight the pattern to hold it in place. With a sharp pencil, carefully trace around the pattern onto the paper. Cut it out.

3 Remove the paper backing from the styrene. Apply the wrong side of the paper or fabric shade material to the sticky styrene. Start at one edge and work across. Often I find it easier to lay the fabric or paper on the tabletop wrong-side-up and stick the styrene to it from above.

4 Carefully cut the embossed paper along the edge of the styrene.

5 Mark the 1/2" seam allowance on the wrong side of one end of the shade. Place a bead of glue inside this marked line. Butt the other end of the shade material to this, overlapping the ends. Clamp the top and bottom edges of the seam with bulldog clips. Clean up any glue seepage. Lay the shade down on a clean surface. Weight the seam with books and allow the glue to dry.

6 When the glue has dried, remove the books and bulldog clips. Apply a thin bead of glue along the top inside edge of the shade, rotating the shade as you do so. Slip the top ring into the shade from the bottom. Fit the ring just inside the top edge. Clamp in place with a bulldog clip at the back seam. Work around the shade, matching the ring and clamping with clips. Clean up any extra glue with a moist paper towel.

7 Turn the shade upside-down and repeat for the bottom ring.

8 To finish your lampshade, cover the raw edges of the styrene and the fitter rings at the top and bottom edges with binding tape as instructed on page 23. Then decorate with the grosgrain ribbon as a flat trim. Use the wider ribbon at the bottom of the shade.

Vase Lamp

You can turn just about any opaque vase into a lamp—fast! Though this Italian art deco vase was too special to drill a hole in its side for the cord to exit, you may wish to do so with your vase. To finish the hole nicely, the mail order lamp suppliers listed at the back of the book can furnish you with a rubber grommet that will fit in the drilled hole.

The item that turns a vase into a lamp is called a vase cap. Available from lamp suppliers in sizes ranging from 1½" to 4½", vase caps have a brass finish. To match the vase, I spray painted mine copper.

Choose your lamp pipe by measuring the inside height of the vase. Add the height of the vase neck (I bought one 1½" tall) and about 3/4" for the height of the vase cap. Err on the short side as you can fill the bottom of the vase with Styrofoam.

If you wish, glue the vase cap to the rim of the vase in step 4. The lip of the vase cap holds snugly to the edge of my vase, so I didn't have to use glue.

MATERIALS

- Vase
- Vase cap to cover opening (see lamp suppliers in Sources)
- Lamp pipe
- Lamp neck
- Spray paint (optional)
- Two washers
- Two nuts
- Large (1½"-wide or so) washer
- Side exit socket
- Cord set
- Styrofoam

INSTRUCTIONS

1 Spray paint the vase cap and neck if desired.

2 Place a piece of Styrofoam in the bottom of the vase, cutting the piece about 2″ tall and wide enough to fit snugly. Screw a nut on one end of the pipe. Add a small washer, then a large, then another small washer, then the other nut. Push this end of the pipe into the vase hard enough to embed it in the Styrofoam. Cut a piece of Styrofoam tall enough to go nearly to the top of the vase and push it down into the vase, poking the lamp pipe in the center as you do. Wedge pieces of Styrofoam tightly into the vase at the sides to secure.

3 Place the vase cap and neck on the lamp pipe and screw the socket cap (threaded bottom part) in place.

4 As instructed on page 12, wire your lamp.

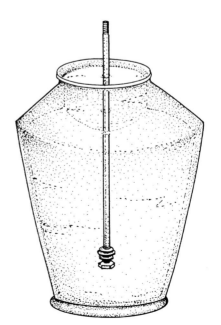

Dollhouse Windows Lampshade

Yes, this lamp is made from four dollhouse windows! Large dollhouse windows, that is. The long edges of the windows are joined by gluing them to a piece of balsa wood. The paper-covered styrene fitted inside each window makes this an oriental-looking shade.

You will need a drill to make holes in the balsa for the bulb clip. The wires on the bulb clip I used were about the size of a 5/64" drill bit. Hold the bit to the wire to judge which size you will need. The ring part of the bulb clip top wire will be cut, so it doesn't matter what size ring you use. I used Delta Fruitwood stain and satin spray varnish for my shade.

MATERIALS

- *Four 24-light panel dollhouse windows #5007 (see Hobby Builders Supply in Sources)*
- *Four 3/8" square pieces of bass wood or balsa, each 8" long for sides*
- *Two 1/4" x 1/2" pieces of basswood or balsa, each 5¾" long for top*
- *Stain*
- *Varnish*
- *Bulb clip top wire (see above)*
- *Pressure-sensitive styrene*
- *Rice paper or handmade paper*
- *Glue*
- *Wood glue*

INSTRUCTIONS

❶ Using wood glue, glue the 3/8" square balsa pieces to the long edges of the windows as shown.

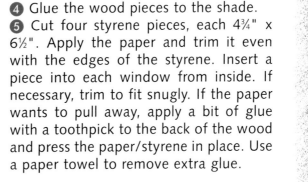

❷ Stain all the wood. Seal with two or three coats of varnish.
❸ Drill holes in one side of each of the two top wood pieces. Center them on the 1/4" thickness of the wood, having them about 1/4" apart. Dab the ends of the wire in glue and insert into the lamp holes.

❹ Glue the wood pieces to the shade.
❺ Cut four styrene pieces, each 4¾" x 6½". Apply the paper and trim it even with the edges of the styrene. Insert a piece into each window from inside. If necessary, trim to fit snugly. If the paper wants to pull away, apply a bit of glue with a toothpick to the back of the wood and press the paper/styrene in place. Use a paper towel to remove extra glue.

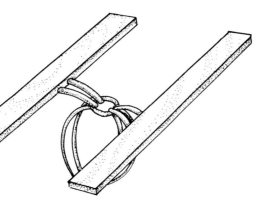

Photo Transfer Lampshade

*U*sing a nifty transfer medium, you can transfer any image to fabric. The best part is, you use a photocopy of the image to transfer so you don't have to ruin the original.

For my shade I chose a black and white woodcut, though the process will work for color copies as well. Simply follow the manufacturer's instructions on the photo transfer medium. You'll be surprised at how easy it is!

MATERIALS

- *7" x 10" x 7" hexagonal lampshade (see Mainely Shades in Sources)*
- *Six photocopies, one for each of the shade panels*
- *Muslin fabric, cut in six pieces larger than each shade panel*
- *Aleene's Transfer-It*
- *Hug Snug (see Sources)*
- *Glue*
- *Black velvet ribbon: 1½ yards 5/8"-wide, 1⅔ yards 1"-wide*

INSTRUCTIONS

❶ Lay one section of the shade frame on the fabric. Trace just outside the wire.

❷ Cut out, leaving about 2" outside the marked lines. Repeat five times to make six panels for the hexagonal shade.

❸ Likewise, lay a frame section over one of the photocopies. Adjust the frame to fit over the picture as you like it. Trace around the frame. Cut out on the traced lines. Repeat for the other five photocopies.

❹ Following the manufacturer's instructions, transfer the image to the fabric pieces inside the marked lines. Don't be sparing in the amount of transfer medium you use.

❺ Wrap the frame with Hug Snug as instructed on page 21.

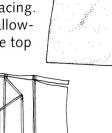

❻ Stitch the panels together with right sides facing. Trim the side seam allowances to 1/4". Trim the top and bottom edges to the marked lines. Glue to the frame.

❼ Glue 5/8"-wide velvet ribbon over the six vertical wires. Glue 1"-wide velvet ribbon over the top and bottom wires as binding as instructed on page 23, making your placement line 1/2" from the top of the wire.

Seat Caning Lampshade

*T*his shade is made from the woven cane used to replace chair seats. The edging is natural reed used for basket making. Leave the shade natural, as I did, or stain, paint, pickle, or whatever strikes your fancy, before constructing the frame.

MATERIALS

- Two feet of pre-woven seat cane webbing (see Constantine's in Sources)
- 7" x 11" oval washer top fitter wire
- 7" x 11" oval bottom fitter wire
- 7" x 30½" pressure-sensitive styrene
- Binding tape
- 5/8" flat reed (see Constantine's in Sources)
- Glue

Find the pattern for this lampshade on page 129.

INSTRUCTIONS

1 Using the pattern on pages 129-130, cut a piece of styrene for the shade.

2 Lay the styrene sticky-side-up on your work surface. Lay the caning on top so the caning is square, parallel to the styrene. Press the caning to the styrene. Trim the caning even with the edge of the styrene.

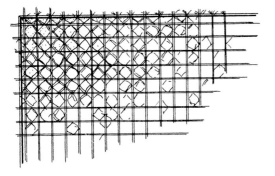

3 To glue the back seam, mark the 1/2" seam allowance on the wrong side of one end of the shade. Place a bead of glue inside this marked line. Butt the other end of the shade material to this, overlapping the ends. Clamp the top and bottom edges of the seam with bulldog clips. Clean up any glue seepage. Lay the shade down on a clean surface. Weight the seam with books and allow the glue to dry.

4 When the glue has dried, remove the books and bulldog clips. Apply a thin bead of glue along the top inside edge of the shade, rotating the shade as you do so. Slip the top ring into the shade from the bottom. Fit the ring just inside the top edge. Clamp in place with bulldog clip at the back seam. Work around the shade, matching the ring and clamping with clips. Clean up any extra glue.

5 Turn the shade upside-down and repeat for the bottom ring.

6 Allow to dry several hours or overnight and remove the bulldog clips.

7 Cover the wires and edges of styrene with cotton twill tape as instructed on page 23.

8 Glue the reed to the top and bottom edges of the frame and clamp with bull clips. Have the top and bottom edges of the reed extend a good 1/8" above and below the wires respectively.

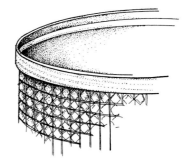

Basket Lampshade

*G*et out your glue gun and turn a basket into a lampshade. It's that easy! To choose the size of the fitter ring, measure the diameter of the inside bottom of the basket (which will be the top of the shade) where the ring will rest.

 Basket
 Clip top fitter ring (see lamp suppliers in Sources)
 Hot glue gun

INSTRUCTIONS

1 Apply hot glue to the fitter ring and insert it into the basket.

Hat Lampshade

*M*ake this feminine shade quickly and with just a few supplies. I found a plain straw hat at a department store. An antique dealer who specializes in wearables supplied the yellow flowers. You may also wish to cover your hat with netting.

MATERIALS

- Hat
- 5" bulb lip fitter ring
- Three yards ribbon
- Flower bunch
- Fine wire
- Hot glue gun
- Glue

INSTRUCTIONS

❶ Apply hot glue to the fitter ring and place it inside the upside-down hat.

❷ Decide where the flowers and ribbon will be on the hat brim. I put mine on the side. Cut a piece of ribbon long enough to go around the hat plus a few inches. Glue the ribbon to the hat, overlapping the ends where the flowers and bow will cover.

❸ Make a bow as illustrated with the remaining ribbon. Secure with wire.

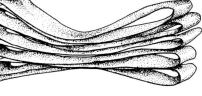

❹ Wrap a piece of wire around the flower bunch and wire the ribbon and flower bunch to the hat. Poke the wire ends inside the hat and twist.

Manuscript Shade

*P*erfect for a desk or den, this lamp celebrates the art of writing. I used a paper from Collage (see Sources) that looks like an old manuscript. You may wish to make copies of old family documents, love letters, or a copy of the Declaration of Independence for your lampshade.

For the sealing wax and stamp, I checked the yellow pages and found a delightful stationer who carries sealing wax and a tempting array of stamps.

MATERIALS

- Decorative paper of your choice
- 8" washer top round fitter ring
- 8" round bottom fitter ring
- Pressure-sensitive styrene
- Two yards binding tape
- Two yards 3/4"-wide trim
- One yard round trim
- One yard 1/4"-wide ribbon
- Package of sealing wax wafers
- Rubber stamp
- Gold pigment ink brush pad
- Glue
- Hot glue gun

Find the pattern for this lampshade on page 131.

INSTRUCTIONS

1 Using the pattern, cut a piece of styrene and clothespin it to the fitter rings. Because fitter rings can vary slightly in size, mark the overlap on the non-paper side (inside) of the styrene. Remove the clothespins.

2 As instructed on page 20, attach the paper to the styrene, glue the back seam, and attach the fitter rings. Bind.

3 Apply the binding tape to the top and bottom of the shade as instructed on page 23.

4 Glue the 3/4"-wide trim to the top and bottom edges of the shade.

5 Prepare the stamp by dabbing it on the gold ink pad. Put a wax wafer on a piece of tin foil. Hold a hair dryer directly over it to soften it. The wafer will scoot away if the dryer isn't directed squarely at it. It will take less than a minute to soften the wax. Turn off the dryer and stamp the wax wafer. Leave the stamp in the wax for a minute or two, then peel the wax from the stamp. Repeat to make nine stamped wafers.

6 Cut the ribbon into 4" pieces. Fold as shown and tack them with glue or thread.

7 Arrange a ruler, the thin round trim, the ribbon pieces, and the stamped wax wafers close by and heat your glue gun. Starting at the back seam of the bottom edge of the shade, hot glue one end of the round trim over the 3/4" trim that is glued to the shade. Glue a piece of the ribbon over the round trim, then glue a stamped wafer on top.

8 Measure to the right 3". Bring the round trim over, letting it hang just a bit. Glue the round trim, then the ribbon and wafer. Repeat around the shade.

Cork Shade

Cork is a natural material that requires only glue to become a nifty lampshade. Cork is available at craft stores and through mail order (see Dick Blick in Sources). Upholstery nails can be found in the home decorating areas of fabric stores.

If the cork pieces are quite curled from being on the roll in the plastic package, you may need to weight them overnight to flatten them for easier handling.

MATERIALS

- **Square shade frame (see #4185 Mainely Shades in Sources)**
- **Roll of cork**
- **Glue**
- **Upholstery nails**
- **Hot glue gun**
- **Craft knife**
- **Wire cutters**

Find the pattern for this lampshade on page 133.

INSTRUCTIONS

❶ Trace the pattern pieces from pages 133-134 onto paper. Trace the trim pattern onto a separate piece of paper. Tape the top piece to the bottom piece to make a complete pattern piece for one side. Lay the taped pattern on the cork and trace around it. With a sharp craft knife and a ruler, cut out just inside the traced lines. Repeat to make the four side pieces. Do the same for the shade trim. Make four short and four long pieces of trim.

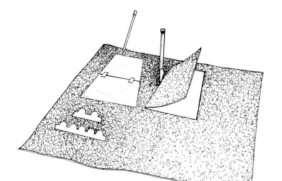

❷ Apply glue to the four sides of one frame section. Apply a piece of cork with the right edge even with the wire and the top and bottom edges extending below the wire by the same amount. Weight with a very large book or box and allow to dry.

❸ Apply glue to the section of the frame to the right of the first section. Glue a second cork section in place, butting the left side up to the first piece of cork as illustrated. Weight until dry. Repeat for the two remaining sections.

❹ Use a craft knife to trim the cork as necessary.

❺ Glue a top and bottom trim piece in place on one cork section, centering them and having the top edge even with the top edge of the cork piece underneath. Weight and allow to dry. Repeat for the three remaining sections.

❻ Using wire cutters, trim the nail ends from the upholstery nails. Hot glue in place.

Dollhouse Shutters Lampshade

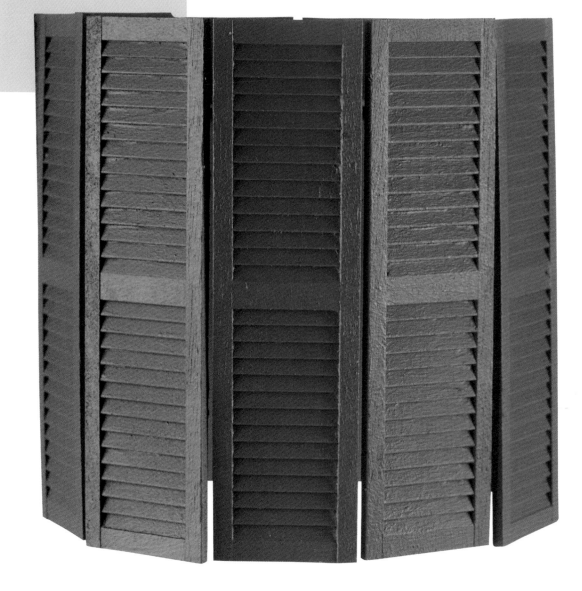

*D*ollhouse shutters are the perfect size for a candlestick lampshade. They come in pairs but the diameter of the fitter ring I used dictated an odd number of shutters. Choose a paint color to suit the room you intend for this little shade. Stain is an option as well.

MATERIALS

- 11 dollhouse shutters 1⁷⁄₁₆" x 5 ⅛" (see #5019 Hobby Builders Supply in Sources)
- Liberty Blue acrylic paint by Delta
- Matte spray varnish
- 5" candle clip round fitter ring
- 5" round bottom fitter ring
- Pressure-sensitive styrene
- Glue
- Hot glue gun

INSTRUCTIONS

❶ Lightly sand the shutters. Remove sanding dust with a tack cloth.

❷ Paint the backs of the shutters with Liberty Blue. When dry, flip over and paint the fronts. Use the tip of the brush to get inside the angled corners of the louvers. Let dry.

❸ Seal with the matte spray varnish, first spraying the backs and allowing to dry, then the fronts. Apply two coats.

❹ Cut a piece of styrene 3½" x 16¾". With the sticky (paper-covered) side, pull back the paper on one short edge of the styrene and overlap the short edges 1/2". Put the fitter ring inside to make sure it fits. Adjust if necessary and glue in place. Glue the fitter ring inside along one edge of the styrene to be the top of the shade.

❺ Lay out the shutters and make sure the louvers all face in one direction. With a piece of chalk, mark the backs of the shutters 3/4" from the top and bottom edges. Arrange the shutters on the styrene, adjusting them evenly. One at a time, remove and hot glue each shutter to the outside of the styrene, making sure the edges of the styrene match the 3/4″ markings on the back of the shutter.

Rubber Stamped Shade

With a rubber stamp in hand, anyone is an artist. Simply stamp the image with waterproof ink, and it's paint by numbers from there!

Choose a smooth paper for the shade. This will produce clean stamped images. Parchment works well. Since the paper I used was nearly white, I antiqued it after stamping. This also softened the brightness of the stamped and colored images. Practice a few stamps on scrap paper before doing the real thing. Test the antiquing on a scrap of the paper to see how much to apply when you work on your final project.

MATERIALS

- 4" round clip top fitter ring
- 8" round fitter ring
- Pressure-sensitive styrene
- Parchment or other smooth paper for stamping
- Rubber stamps from Rubber Stampede (see Sources):
    - Chrysanthemum #A1661H
    - Pansy #A1667H
    - Poppy #A1664H
    - Victorian Butterfly Collection #951.57
- Waterproof ink stamp pad
- Watercolor markers
- Warm Brown antiquing gel from Delta
- Spray sealer/finish
- 1/2 yard binding tape
- 1/2 yard trim
- Glue

Find the pattern for this lampshade on page 135.

INSTRUCTIONS

❶ Make the shade pattern as instructed on page 135. To determine the placement for the three flower stamps, fold the pattern in half down the center and in half again. The three folds are the placement lines.

❷ Trace the pattern onto the styrene and cut out.

❸ Adhere the paper to the styrene. Trim to about 1" all around. Lay the shade pattern on the paper. Mark the top and bottom of the three placement folds.

❹ To apply ink to a large flower stamp, hold the stamp rubber-side-up and tap the ink pad on the stamp. Center the stamp between the placement marks and press it on the paper. Do the same for the other two flower stamps. Add some butterflies. Let dry.

❺ Referring to the colored images on the backs of the stamps, fill in the stamped images with watercolor pens. Let dry.

❻ Spray with one coat of sealer. Let dry.

❼ Water down some antiquing gel. Using a piece of paper towel, lightly dab antiquing gel on the shade. Blot it first. To achieve a soft effect, dab with a clean paper towel when still wet. Allow to dry.

❽ Apply two coats of sealer, allowing drying time between the coats.

❾ Trim the shade paper even with the edges of the styrene at top and bottom. On the short sides, trim to 1/2" and press and glue to the back of the styrene.

❿ Refer to page 20 to finish the shade and apply the binding and trim.

Confetti Lampshade

*T*his cheerful little shade is easy to make. You may choose tissue paper dot colors to suit your candlestick. If you find only off-white pompom fringe as I did, grab a bottle of dye while you're at the store. I used hot water and salt in my bathroom sink to dye the fringe. Let it soak for close to 30 minutes, stirring a few times to make sure all parts of the fringe are dyed. Rinse well, squeeze the water out, then pop the fringe in the dryer.

MATERIALS

- *4" candle clip round fitter ring*
- *5" round bottom fitter ring*
- *Pressure-sensitive styrene*
- *White tissue paper*
- *Tissue paper in desired colors*
- *Spray mount*
- *Mod Podge (or thinned white craft glue)*
- *One yard pompom trim*

Find the pattern for this lampshade on page 137.

INSTRUCTIONS

1 Cut the colored tissue paper into workable-size pieces, roughly 4". Stack them. Using a hole punch, punch the tissue. It will be easier if you put the stacked tissue paper between two sheets of regular paper. Separate the colored circles and throw out the white paper circles. (Unless you want to use them!)

2 Make a shade pattern as instructed on page 137.

3 Trace the pattern onto styrene. Mark the 1/2" line for the side seam overlap on the non-paper side and cut out.

4 Crumple a piece of white tissue paper. Remove the paper from the styrene. Attach the crumpled white tissue paper to the styrene.

5 Spray the tissue paper with spray mount. One-by-one, place the colored tissue paper dots on the white tissue paper. I chose to concentrate dots at the bottom of my shade.

6 Spray again with spray mount. Crumple another piece of white tissue paper and press on top.

7 Trim the tissue paper around the edges of the styrene to 1/2". At the short side edges, turn and glue the back.

8 Match one short edge to the line at the side seam and glue the seam. Clamp and let dry.

9 Glue the fitter rings in place as instructed on page 20.

10 Turn the extra tissue paper at the top and bottom to the back.

11 Apply thinned Mod Podge to the tissue paper shade.

12 Hot glue the pompom fringe to the top and bottom edges of the shade.

Super Easy Candlestick Lamps

*T*hanks to the lamp suppliers in the Sources section at the back of the book, it takes mere minutes to turn a candlestick into a lamp.

All you need is an opaque candlestick and an electric candlestick adapter. The adapter is supplied with a rubber end that goes in the hole for the candle. To make it fit your candle, unscrew the rubber and then rub it on coarse sandpaper until it fits snugly in the candlestick. Add a shade and voila! You have a little lamp.

About The Author

As the author of well over a dozen crafts books, Jodie Davis regards herself as lucky. Lucky to combine her love of creating with the profession of writing.

Jodie is self-taught as both a designer and writer, having delved into many creative venues from early on. True to form, when she got the notion to write her first book, she headed for the library to find out how.

Writing *Crafting Lamps & Shades* provided the opportunity for Jodie to share her love of such diverse crafts as rubber stamping and decorative painting.

Jodie grew up in New England, lived in Northern Virginia for over a decade, and now enjoys the discoveries presented by her new home in tropical Coral Springs, Florida.

Sources

ADD YOUR TOUCH
P.O. Box 570
Ripon, WI 54971
(920) 748-6777
I found the birdhouse/lighthouse for the lamp base at a national crafts chain. If you can't find one locally, the company offers mail order. They also carry a number of other intriguing wood products.

ANTHONY WOOD PRODUCTS
113 Industrial Loop
P.O. Box 1081
Hillsboro, TX 76645
(800) 969-2181
Call for a catalog to order the Victorian gingerbread brackets for your lamp base.

AVALON GARDEN
200 Wildwood Road
Hendersonville, NC 28739
(800) 854-0880
www.avalongarden.com
I found the hopping bunny doorstop on Avalon Garden's Web site. They make all sorts of garden ornaments. Not your ordinary local garden center fare!

CHERRY TREE TOYS, INC.
P.O. Box 369
Belmont, OH 43718
(800) 848-4363
www.cherrytree-online.com
You will find the wooden wheels used for the Stacked Boxes and the Victorian Gingerbread lamps as well as other small wooden items in this company's catalog.

COLLAGE
240 Valley Drive
Brisbane, CA 94005
(800) 926-5524
The beautiful papers in the pages of this catalog will inspire you to make paper lampshades. I used several of Collage's papers, including the script paper for the Manuscript Shade.

CONSTANTINE'S
2050 Eastchester Rd.
Bronx, NY 10461
(800) 223-8087
I ordered supplies for the Seat Caning and Brass Chicken Wire shades from Constantine's huge catalog of great woodworking products.

CR'S CRAFTS
P.O. Box 8
Leland, IA 50453
(515) 567-3652
Lots of general crafts supplies at great prices.

CRAFT KING
P.O. Box 90637
Lakeland, FL 33804
(800) 769-9494
Discount crafts supplies.

DELTA TECHNICAL COATINGS, INC.
2550 Pellissier Place
Whittier, CA 90601-1505
(800) 423-4135
www.deltacrafts.com
Delta kindly supplied many of the paints and varnishes I used on my lamps and shades. All of their products are stocked by most craft stores.

DICK BLICK
P.O. Box 1267
Galesburg, IL 61402-1267
(800) 933-2542
Dick Blick has an enormous catalog of every imaginable kind of arts and crafts product. I obtained the tissue paper for sailboat lampshade and brass tooling foil for the flowers for the Strawberry Jar Lamp from this company. Get out a piece of paper and make a wish list!

DUNCAN CRAFTS
5673 E. Shields Ave.
Fresno, CA 93727
(800) 438-6226
www.duncan-enterprise.com
This company manufactures Aleene's Enhancers Mosaic crackle medium which I used for the Victorian Gingerbread Lamp. You will find it on the shelves of your local craft store.

THE ELBRIDGE COMPANY
6110 Merriam Lane
Merriam, KS 66203
(888) 384-4401
The wooden lampshade I stenciled with lace is handmade by this company. They also make other shade styles and a number of intriguing-looking wooden lamp bases.

G & J WHOLESALE LAMP PARTS
4199 State Road 144
Mooresville, IN 46158-9382
(317) 831-1452
This catalog offers an excellent assortment of lamp making supplies.

HOBBY BUILDERS SUPPLY
P.O. Box 921012
Norcross, GA 30092-7012
(800) 926-6464
www.miniatures.com
I found the dollhouse windows and shutters for lampshades in this fun catalog. Order it and enter the world of miniatures!

JERRY'S ARTARAMA
P.O. Box 58638
Raliegh, NC 27658
(800) 827-8478
www.jerrycatalog.com
Some of the handmade paper I used came from my local Jerry's store. The catalog carries some papers as well as many arts and crafts supplies.

THE LAMP SHOP

P.O. Box 3606
Concord, NH 03302-3606
(603) 224-1603

You will find lamp and shade making supplies in this catalog as well as excellent instruction booklets for some of the more traditional lampshade styles.

MAINELY SHADES

100 Gray Road
Falmouth, ME 04105
(800) 554-1755
www.mainelyshades.com

This company offers an excellent array of lamp and shade making supplies. They have the most extensive supply of shade frames I found. Check out their colorful Web site— the catalog is there.

OAK RIDGE FARMS, INC.

P.O. Box 28
Basking Ridge, NJ 07920
(800) 444-8843
www.oakridgefarms.com/orfmap/htm

What beautiful dried flowers! Oak Ridge Farms supplied the hydrangea for the Basket Lamp and dried flowers and moss for Teapot Lamp. The quality is superb.

RUBBER STAMPEDE

P.O. Box 246
Berkley, CA 94701
(800) 632-8386

You may find the stamps I used in your local craft store. If not, contact the company and they will direct you to a source.

WALNUT HOLLOW FARM

Woodcraft Store
1409 State Road 23
Dodgeville, WI 53533
(800) 950-5101

This is the manufacturer of much of the unfinished wood crafts products I see in the chain craft stores. They have a store and mail order service just in case you need something you can't find locally.

Patterns

Bobbin/Trivet Shade

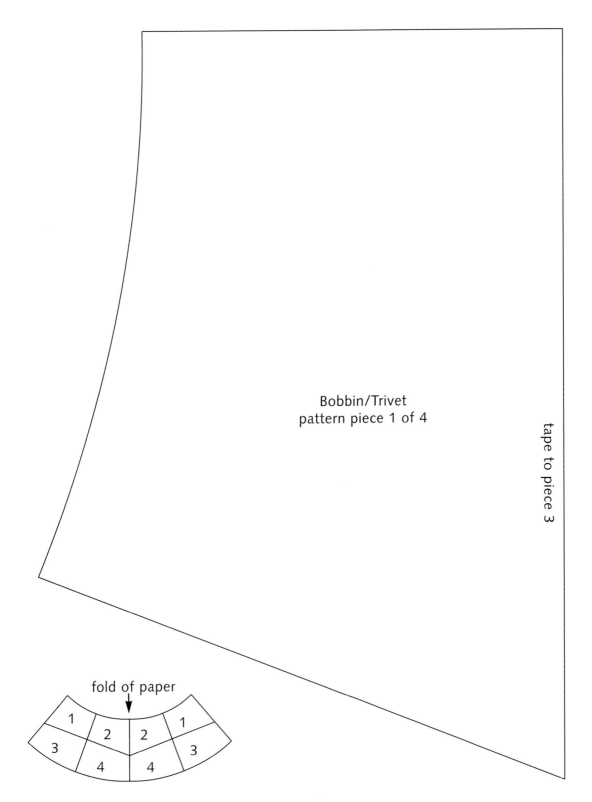

Bobbin/Trivet
pattern piece 1 of 4

tape to piece 3

fold of paper

1
2
2
1
3
3
4
4

Copy patterns from book and cut out. Tape pieces 1 and 2, then 3 and 4 together. Tape 1/2 to 3/4. Place on fold of large paper where indicated on pattern and cut out.

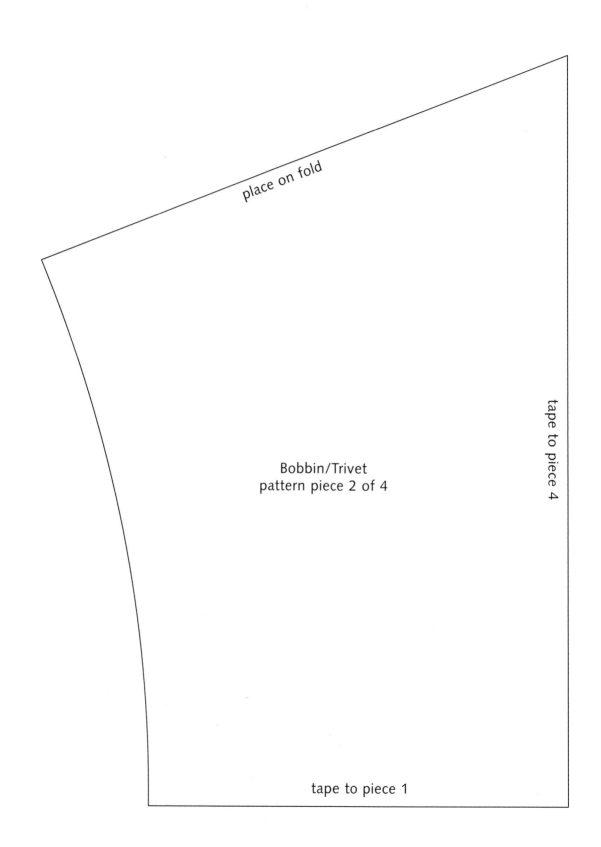

place on fold

tape to piece 4

Bobbin/Trivet
pattern piece 2 of 4

tape to piece 1

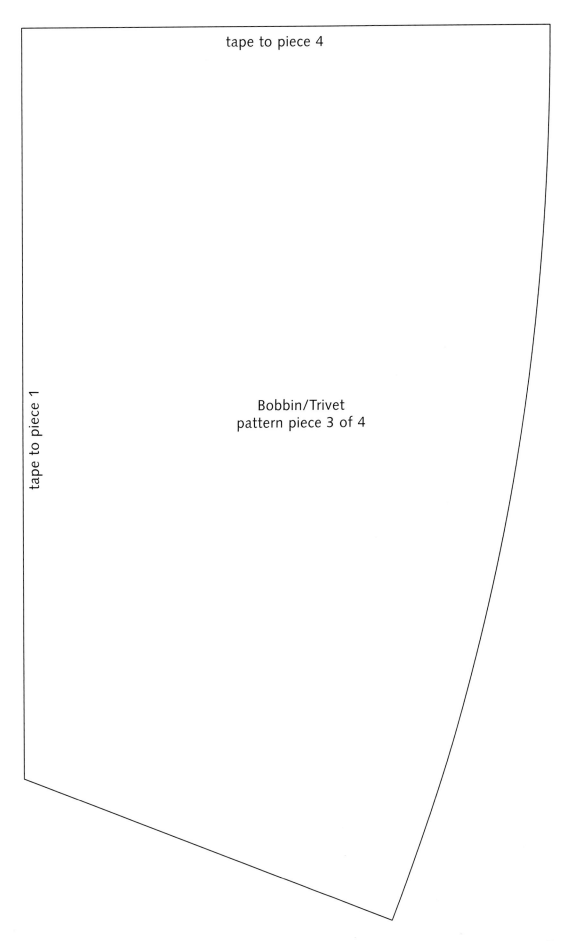

tape to piece 4

tape to piece 1

Bobbin/Trivet
pattern piece 3 of 4

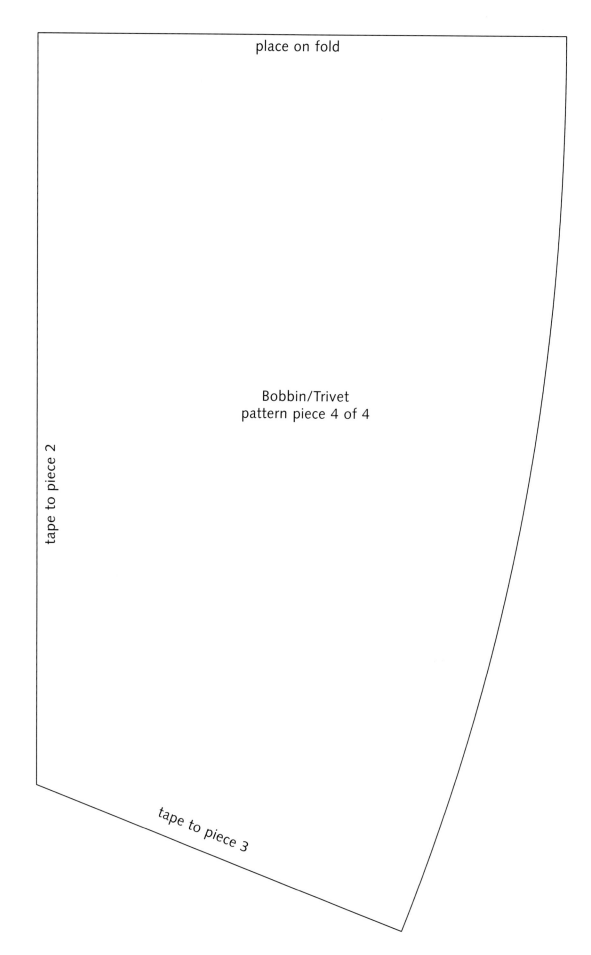

place on fold

Bobbin/Trivet
pattern piece 4 of 4

tape to piece 2

tape to piece 3

Torn Paper Sailboat Shade

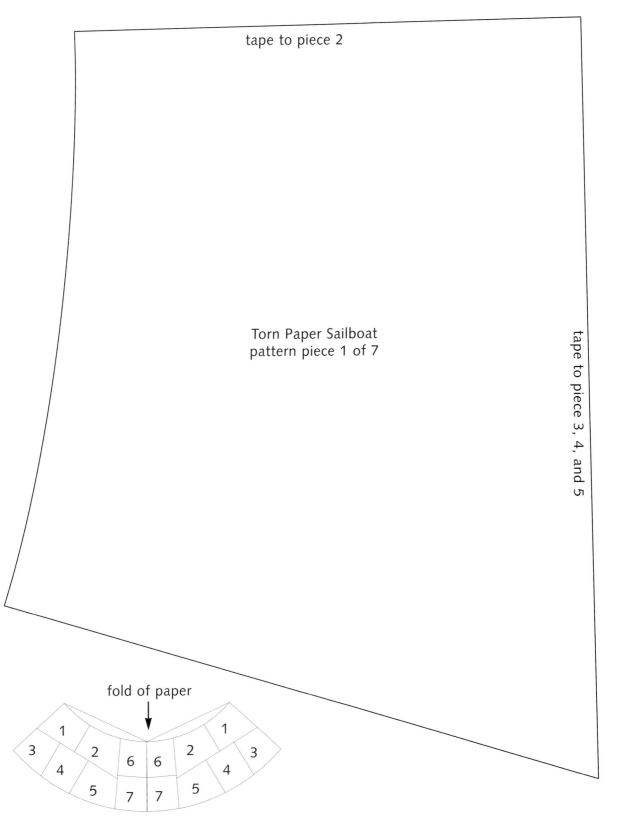

tape to piece 2

Torn Paper Sailboat
pattern piece 1 of 7

tape to piece 3, 4, and 5

fold of paper

Copy patterns from book and cut out. Tape pieces 3, 4, and 5 together. Tape pieces 1 and 2 together, then tape to 3/4/5. Tape pieces 6 and 7 together, then tape to 1/2/3/4/5. To complete the pattern, place the edge indicated on the fold of large paper and cut out.

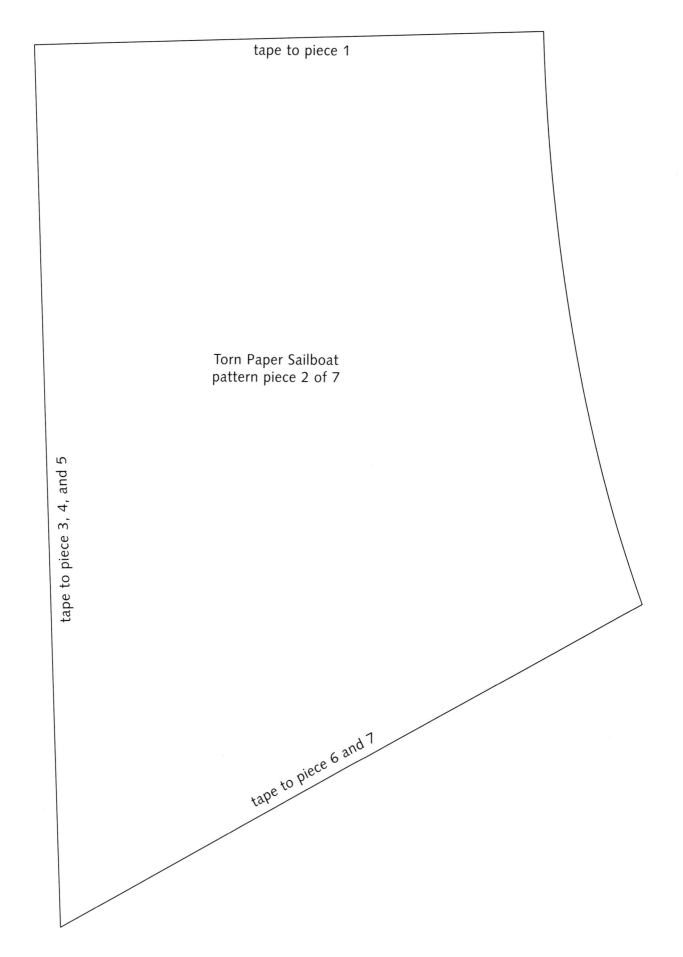

tape to piece 1

Torn Paper Sailboat
pattern piece 2 of 7

tape to piece 3, 4, and 5

tape to piece 6 and 7

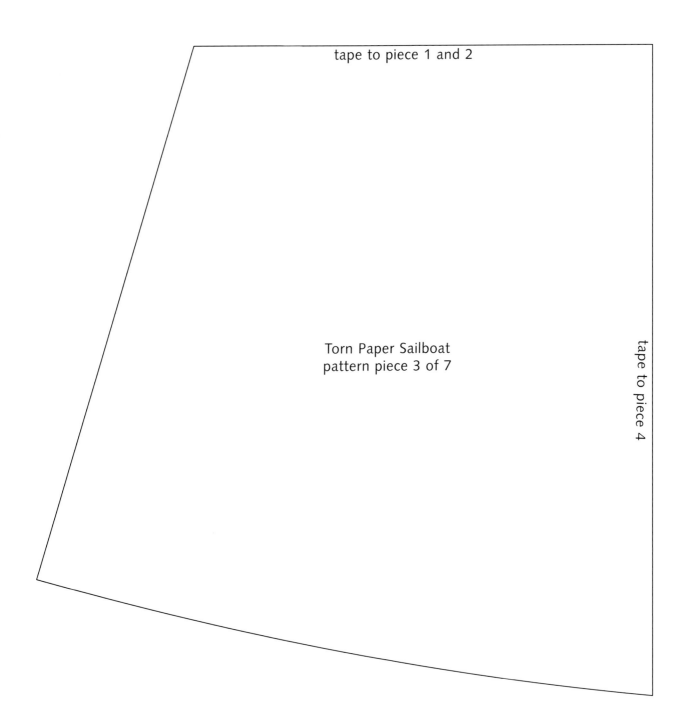

tape to piece 1 and 2

tape to piece 4

Torn Paper Sailboat
pattern piece 3 of 7

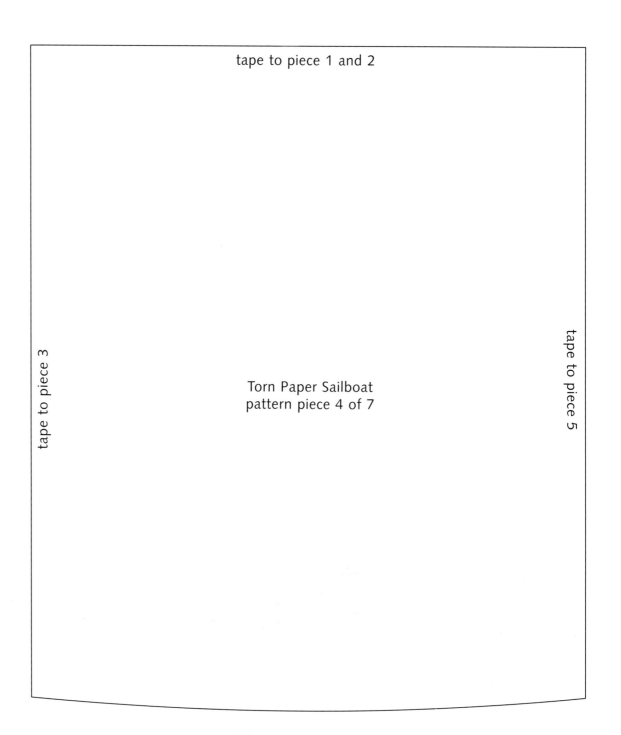

tape to piece 1 and 2

tape to piece 3

tape to piece 5

Torn Paper Sailboat
pattern piece 4 of 7

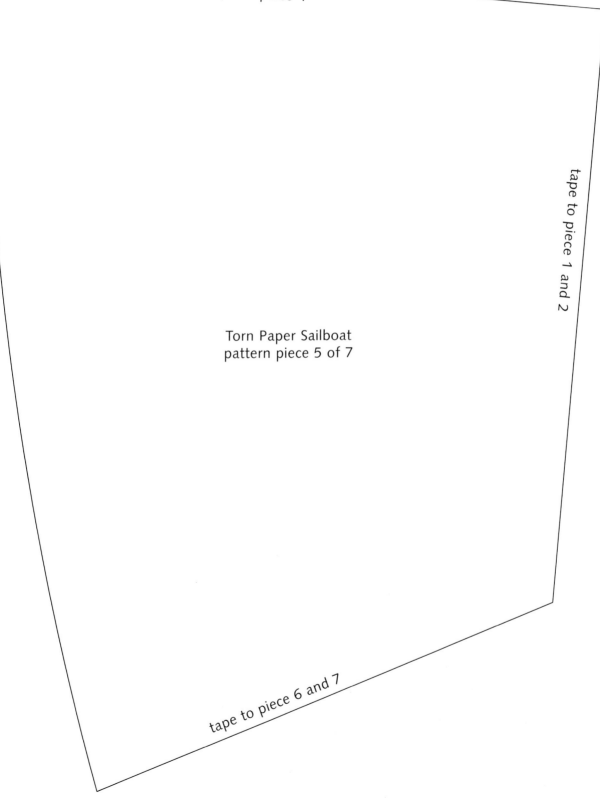

tape to piece 4

tape to piece 1 and 2

Torn Paper Sailboat
pattern piece 5 of 7

tape to piece 6 and 7

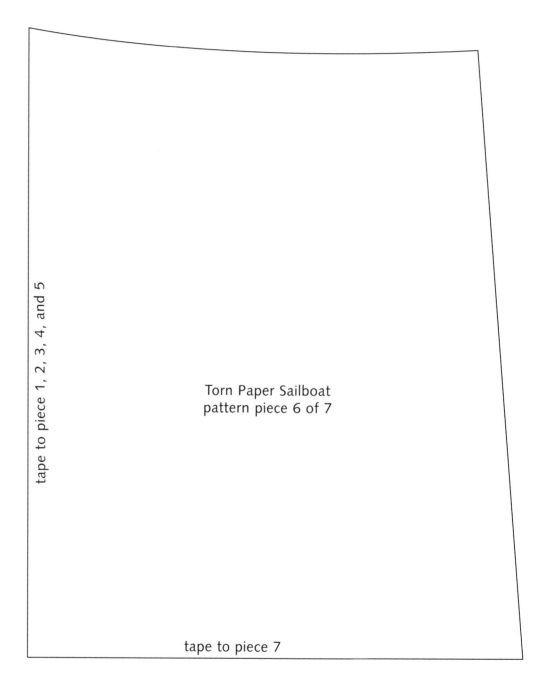

tape to piece 1, 2, 3, 4, and 5

Torn Paper Sailboat
pattern piece 6 of 7

tape to piece 7

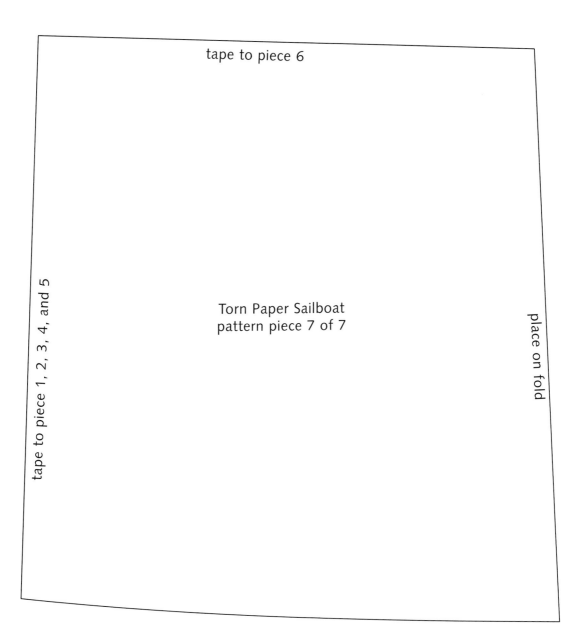

tape to piece 6

tape to piece 1, 2, 3, 4, and 5

Torn Paper Sailboat
pattern piece 7 of 7

place on fold

Dried Flower Shade

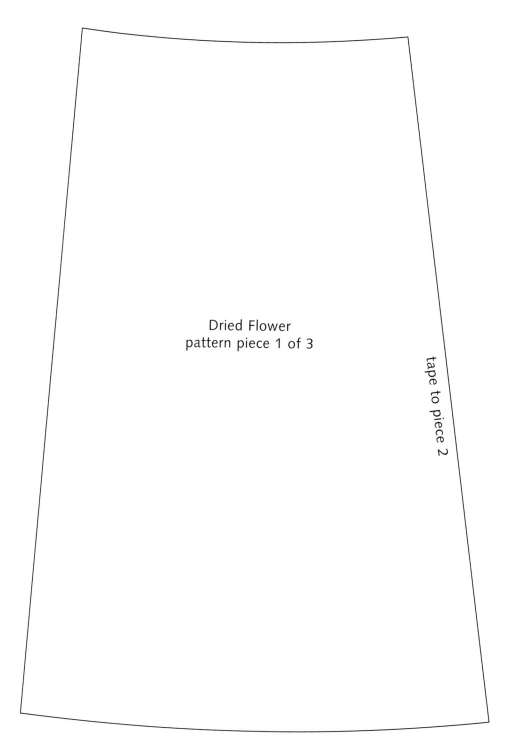

Dried Flower
pattern piece 1 of 3

tape to piece 2

fold of paper

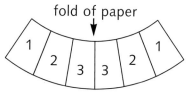

Copy patterns from book and cut out. Tape pieces 1, 2, and 3 together. Place on fold of large paper where indicated on pattern and cut out.

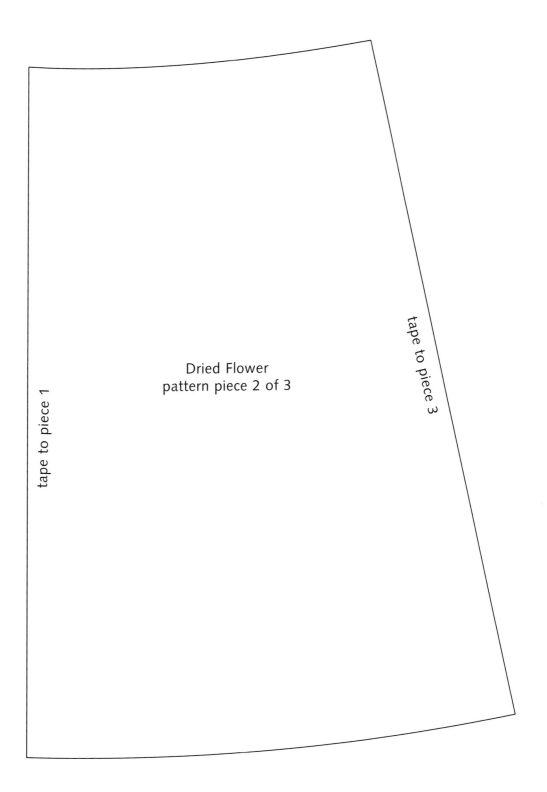

tape to piece 1

Dried Flower
pattern piece 2 of 3

tape to piece 3

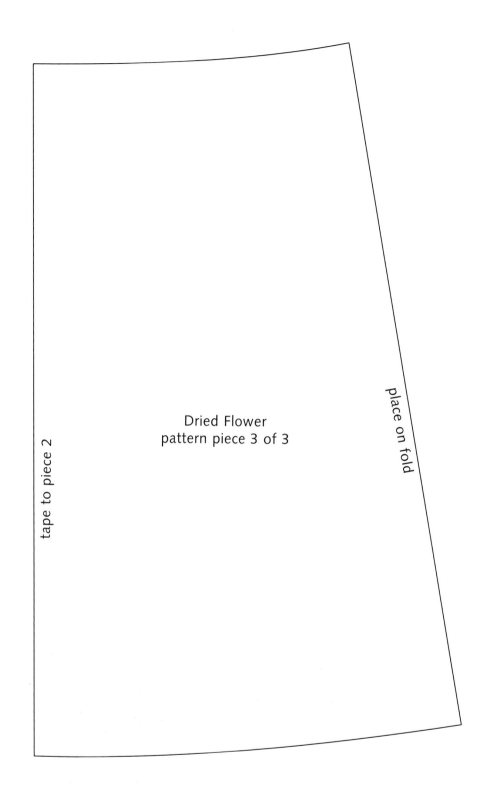

Dried Flower
pattern piece 3 of 3

tape to piece 2

place on fold

Strawberry Jar Lamp

Blue Flower
cut 6, base coat with Emperor Blue

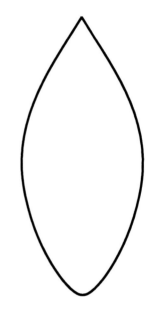

Leaf
cut 18, base coat with True Green

Red Flower
cut 6, base coat with Red Red

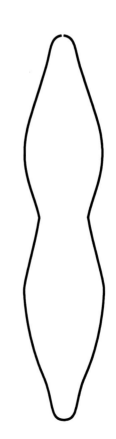

Yellow Flower
cut 18, base coat with Citrus Yellow

Chicken Wire Shade

Chicken Wire
pattern piece 1 of 2

| 1 |
| 1 |
| 1 |
| 2 |

Copy patterns from book and cut out. Cut three of piece 1 and tape them together. Cut one piece 2 and tape to piece 1 set.

Chicken Wire
pattern piece 2 of 2

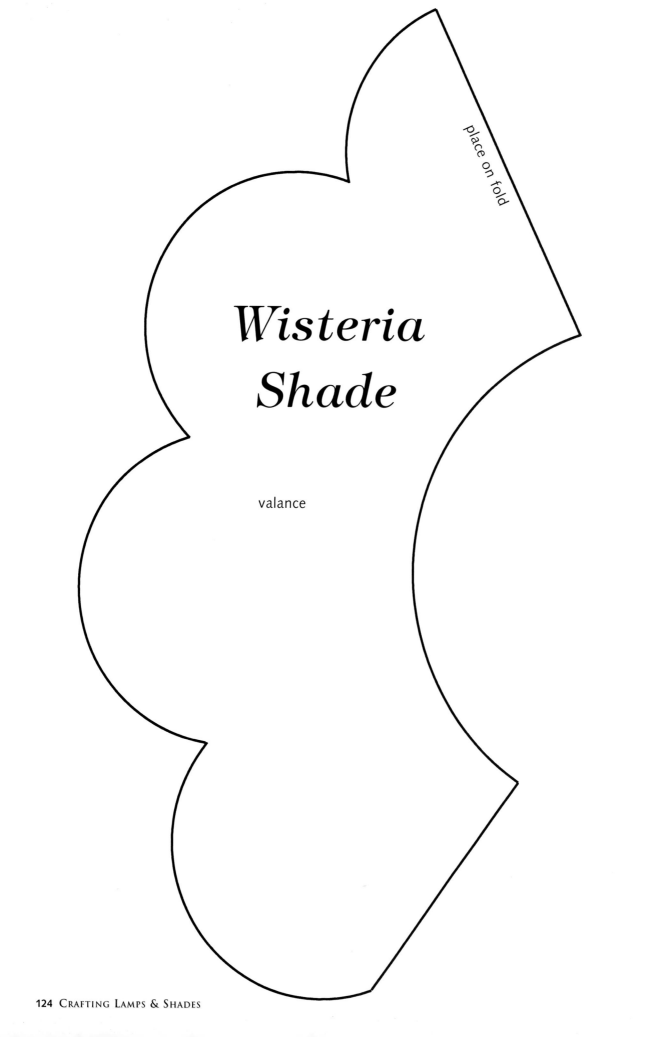

place on fold

Wisteria Shade

valance

Embossed Wallpaper Shade

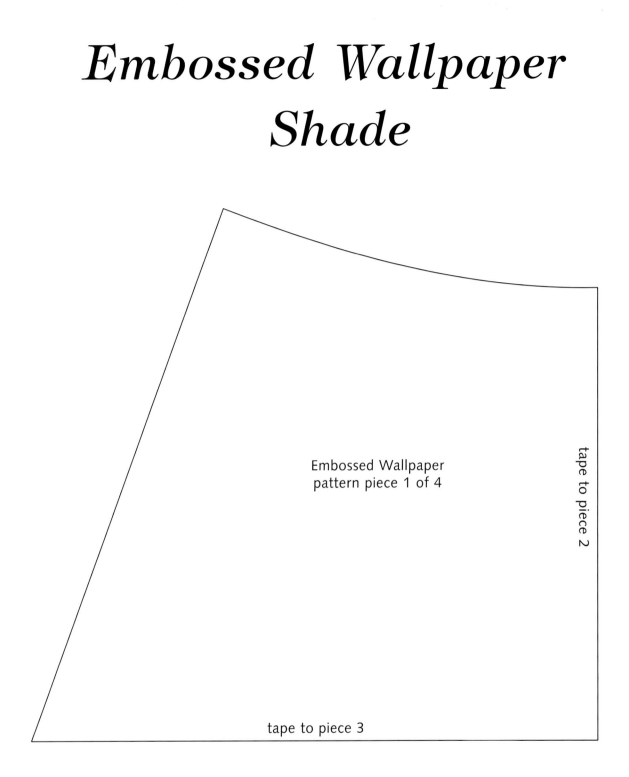

Embossed Wallpaper
pattern piece 1 of 4

tape to piece 2

tape to piece 3

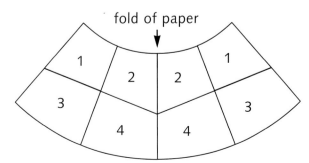

fold of paper

1 2 2 1

3 4 4 3

Copy patterns from book and cut out. Tape pieces 1 and 2, then 3 and 4 together. Tape 1/2 to 3/4. Place pattern edge on fold of large paper where indicated on pattern and cut out.

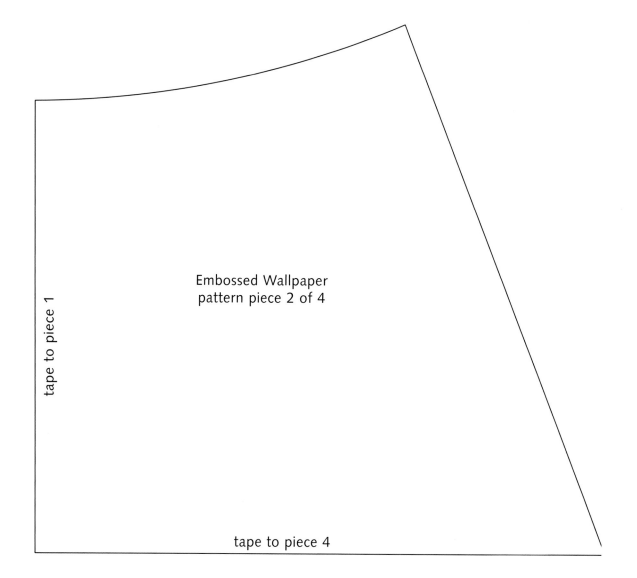

Embossed Wallpaper
pattern piece 2 of 4

tape to piece 1

tape to piece 4

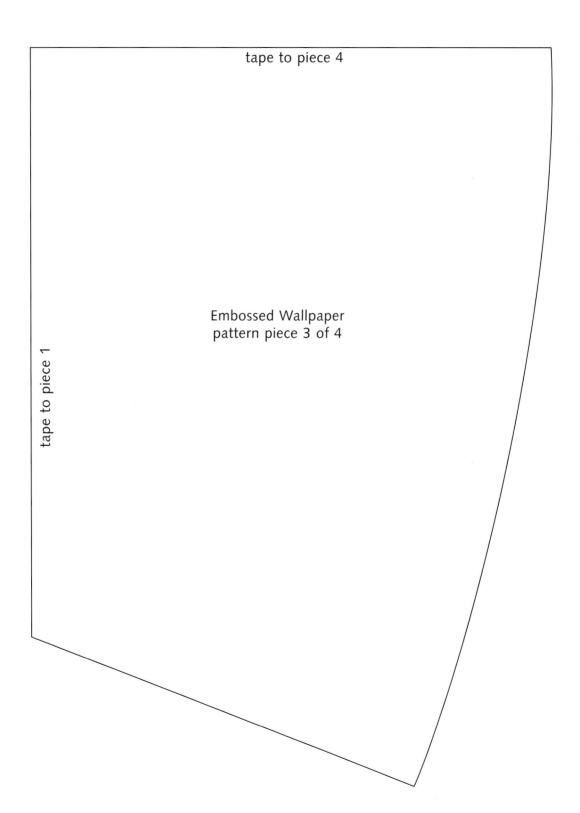

tape to piece 4

tape to piece 1

Embossed Wallpaper
pattern piece 3 of 4

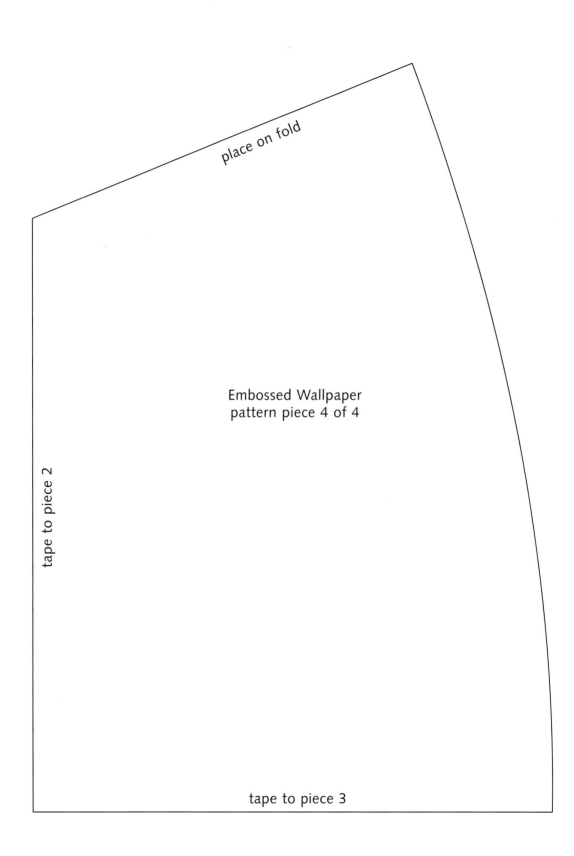

place on fold

Embossed Wallpaper
pattern piece 4 of 4

tape to piece 2

tape to piece 3

Seat Caning Shade

Seat Caning
pattern piece 1 of 2

1	Copy patterns from book and cut out. Cut three of piece 1 and tape them together. Cut one piece 2 and tape to piece 1 set.
1	
1	
2	

Seat Caning
pattern piece 2 of 2

Manuscript Shade

Manuscript
pattern piece 1 of 2

1	1	1	2

Copy patterns from book and cut out. Cut four of piece 1 and tape them together. Cut one piece 2 and tape to piece 1 set.

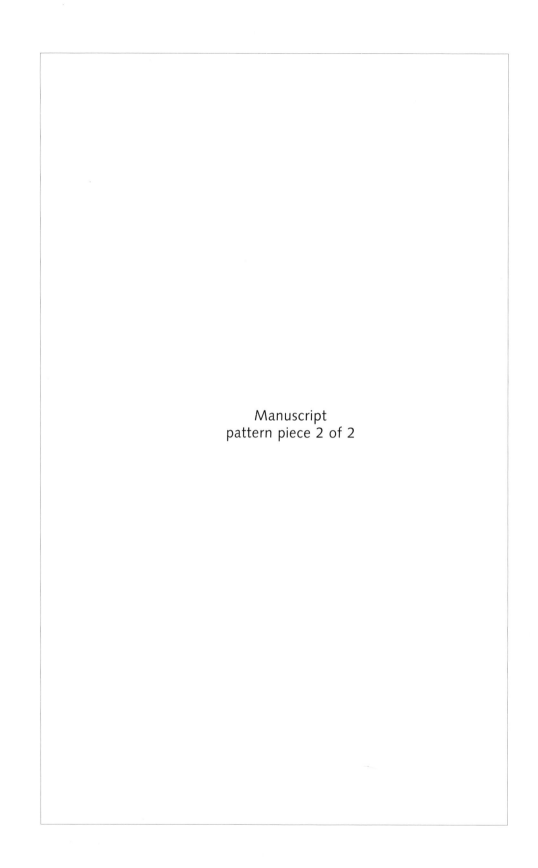

Manuscript
pattern piece 2 of 2

Cork Shade

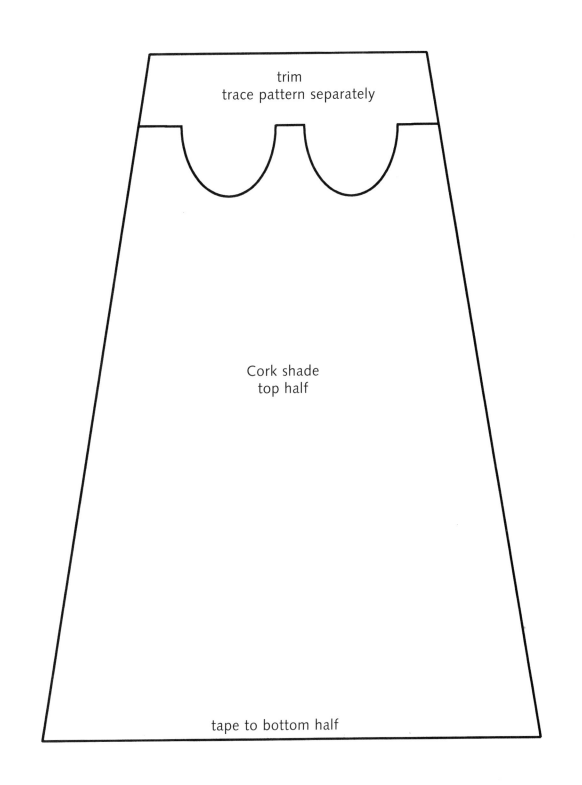

trim
trace pattern separately

Cork shade
top half

tape to bottom half

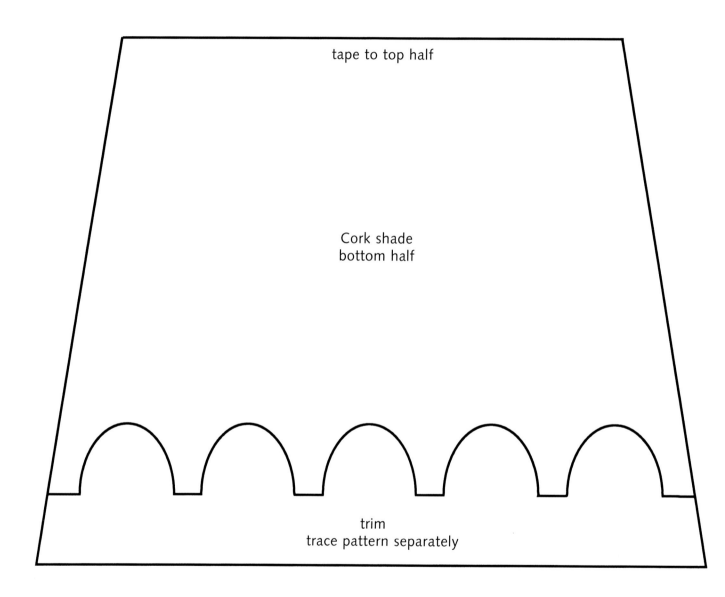

tape to top half

Cork shade
bottom half

trim
trace pattern separately

Rubber Stamped Shade

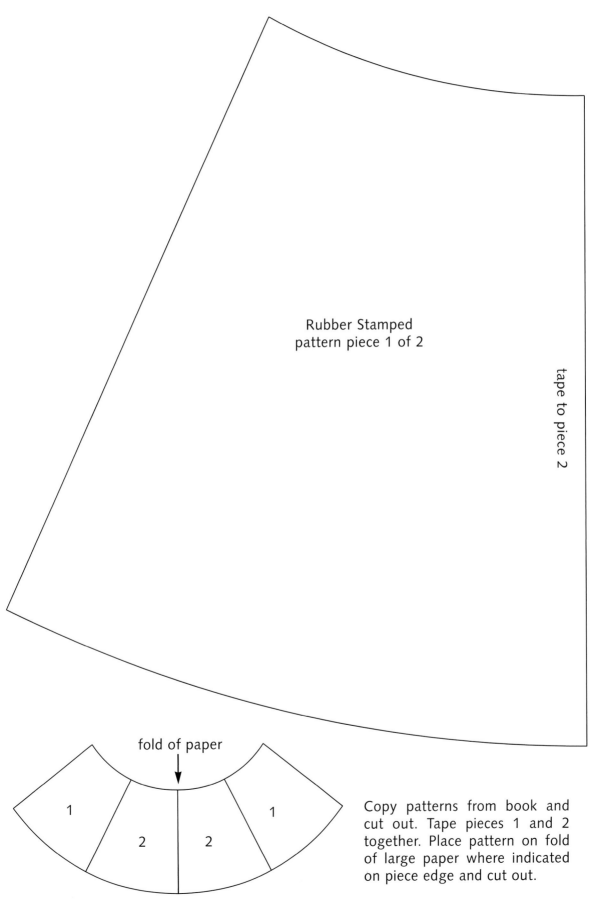

Rubber Stamped
pattern piece 1 of 2

tape to piece 2

fold of paper

1

2

2

1

Copy patterns from book and cut out. Tape pieces 1 and 2 together. Place pattern on fold of large paper where indicated on piece edge and cut out.

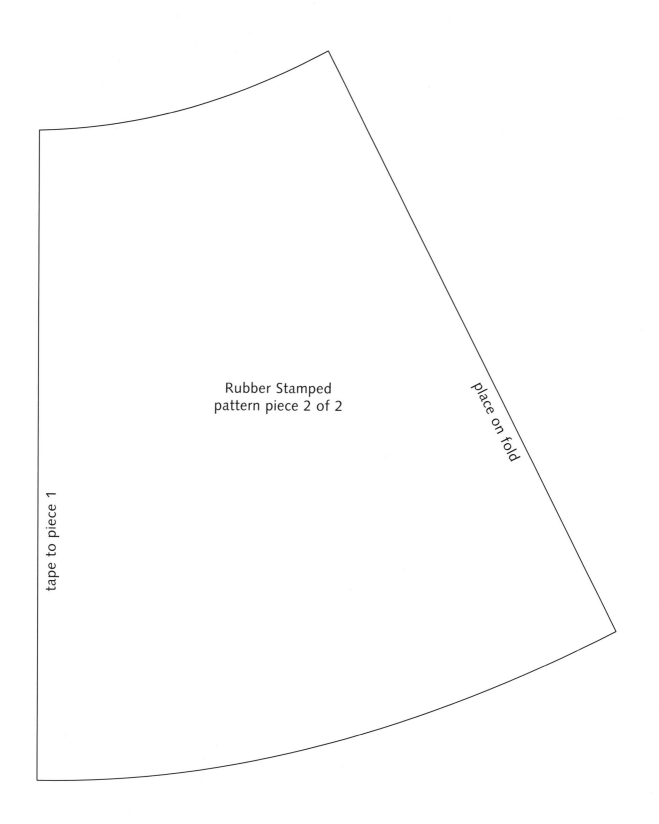

Rubber Stamped
pattern piece 2 of 2

place on fold

tape to piece 1

Confetti Shade

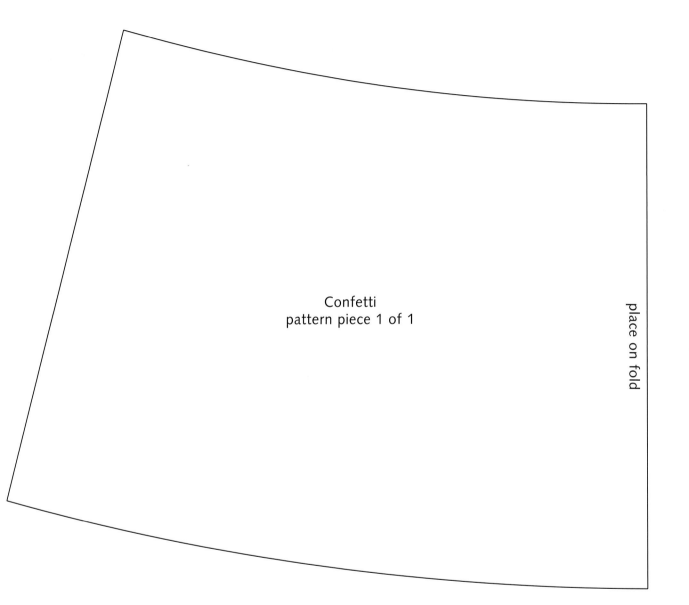

Confetti
pattern piece 1 of 1

place on fold

fold of paper

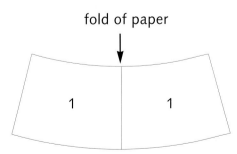

1   1

Copy patterns from book and cut out. Place pattern on folded paper, lining edge on fold as indicated. Cut out.

*I*ndex

Hundreds of Creative Ideas at your Fingertips

PAPER PLUS

Unique Projects Using Handmade Paper

BY NANCY WORRELL

Enter the exciting world of creative papermaking with this detailed guide. Simple step-by-step instructions walk the user through sheetmaking, handcasting and sculpting with a variety of papers. This start-to-finish guide puts the art of papermaking at your fingertips.

Softcover • 8-1/4 x 10-7/8 • 128 pages
80 illustrations • 50 color photos - CHPP • $18.95

FINISHING TOUCHES

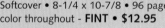

Sewing Decorative Accessories for Your Home
Step-by-step instructions make it easy for you to craft table-linen items, kitchen accessories, picture frames, lampshades, curtains and other window treatments, towels, bedroom ensembles, shower curtains, bows and other flourishes.

Softcover • 8-1/4 x 10-7/8 • 96 pages
color throughout - FINT • $12.95

THE COMPLETE STEP-BY-STEP GUIDE TO HOME SEWING

by Jeanne Argent
Lavishly illustrated with full-color photos, this book is packed with practical suggestions and clear, step-by-step diagrams that show you exactly how to make draperies, curtains and blinds, bed linens, table linens and even elegant, tailored lampshades.

Softcover • 8-1/4 x 10-7/8
• 240 pages - color throughout - CGHS • $24.95

STAMPCRAFT

Dozens of Creative Ideas for Stamping on Cards, Clothing, Furniture, and More
BY CARI HAYSOM
Any surface is up for grabs with stamping. Large and small-scale objects alike take on new dimensions when customized stamping takes over. See just how easy and versatile stamping is with these 40 examples, perfect for beginners and stampaholics alike.

Softcover • 8-1/4 x 10-7/8
• 128 pages - color throughout
STCR • $19.95

THE ART AND CRAFT OF PAPER SCULPTURE

A Step-by-Step Guide to Creating 20 Outstanding and Original Paper Projects
BY PAUL JACKSON
A comprehensive introduction for beginners, inspiration for experienced crafters. You'll learn to create stunning dimensional images in paper with projects from framed relief pictures to mobiles. Simple instructions illustrated by full-color photos.

Softcover • 8-1/4 x 10-7/8
• 128 pages - color throughout
ACPS • $19.95

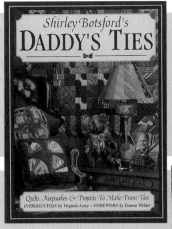
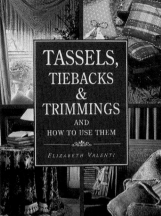

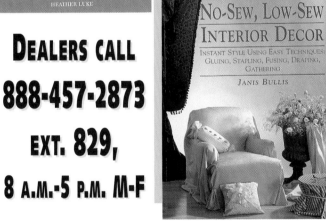
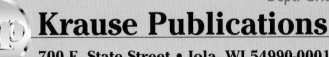

Discover Endless Projects and Add Your Creative Touches

SEW & GO BABY

A Collection of Practical Baby Gear Projects
by Jasmine Hubble
Sew & Go Baby presents 30 practical projects for you to assemble a memorable gift or party for the special baby or toddler in your life. Clear directions, easy-to-follow patterns and full-color photography will enable you to create an entire baby-shower, essential baby gear, clothes, accessories and thoughtful sibling gifts.

NEW

Softcover • 8-1/4 x 10-7/8 • 96 pages
300 Illustrations • 75 color photos
SFTB • $19.95

SEW THE ESSENTIAL WARDROBE FOR 18-INCH DOLLS

Complete Instructions & Full Size Patterns for 18 Modern Outfits
by Joan Hinds & Jean Becker
Dress your doll for any occasion-from a holiday party to a workout at the gym. Authors have designed 18 modern outfits for today's popular 18-inch dolls. Step-by-step instructions are illustrated with helpful diagrams, clear and easy-to-follow sewing instructions, and beautiful color photos for lots of inspiration. Full-size patterns are printed on two convenient pull-outs.

NEW

Softcover • 8-1/4 x 10-7/8 • 96 pages
250 Diagrams • 45 color photos
EWD • $19.95

ADVENTURES WITH POLARFLEECE

A Sewing Expedition
by Nancy Cornwell
Allow author Nancy Cornwell to lead you on a sewing expedition. Explore and discover endless project possibilities for the entire family. Sew a collection of fifteen projects for play, work, fashion, comfort and warmth. The heart of a fallen-away sewer will soon be recaptured and new sewers will be intrigued and inspired.

Softcover • 8-1/2 x 11 • 160 pages
150 Illustrations • 200 photographs
AWPF • $19.95

MORE RIBBON EMBROIDERY BY MACHINE

by Marie Duncan & Betty Farrell
Nineteen exciting projects using the popular ribbon embroidery by machine decorating method. Baby wearables to elegant evening bags are detailed in this instructional volume. Includes how to embellish ready-made items as well as techniques for incorporating beading and heirloom sewing. Sound advice for beginner and expert alike.

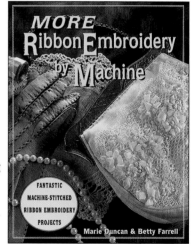

Softcover • 8-1/4 x 10-7/8 • 96 pages
100 color photos
BCUR • $21.95

FOR A **FREE COPY** OF OUR CATALOG PLEASE CALL
800-258-0929
Dept. GNB1

Credit Card Orders Call Toll-free
800-258-0929 Dept. GNB1
Monday-Friday, 7 a.m. - 8 p.m. • Saturday, 8 a.m. - 2 p.m., CST
Visit and order from our secure web site: www.krause.com
Krause Publications • 700 E. State Street • Iola, WI 54990-0001

Dealers call **888-457-2873** ext. **880**   8 a.m. - 5 p.m. M-F

*C*reate a Treasured Collection with the Help of These Books

THE COMPLETE MINIATURE QUILT BOOK
Over 24 Projects for Quilters and Doll Enthusiasts
by Dinah Travis
Hand-made miniature quilts add a touch of interest to your home. Create 25 charming designs suitable for framing, a dolls' bed, hanging or to give as an extraordinary gift. Miniatures are an economical way to try color combinations and experimenting with new designs - little is invested in time and fabric!
Softcover • 10-7/8 x 8-3/8 • 112 pages • 35 b&w photos
50 photos and 20 illustrations • **MINQU** • **$19.95**

NEW

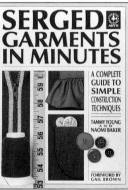

THE ULTIMATE SCRAP QUILT
The Complete Guide to Constructed Fabric
by Joyce Mori
This book opens the door for quilters of all levels to create their own unique fabric by recycling scraps. Incorporating designs such as Amish Triangles and Painted Stars step-by-step instructions for more than 15 finished projects are detailed, complete with time-saving tips and fresh fabric ideas.
Softcover • 8-1/4 x 10-7/8 • 128 pages
70 color photos and 90 color illustrations with b&w templates
USQ • **$21.95**

SNAZAROO ZOO
Great Faces and Easy Costumes to Bring out the Animal in You
by Janis Bullis
Your kids will be wild about this dress-up zoo! One-piece patterns and face painting instructions for 18 different animal costumes are easy to follow and simple to make. Turn basic sweatsuits into frolicking fun with quick cutting and sewing. Includes instructions for accessories such as trunks, tails and antennas.
Softcover • 8-1/4 x 10-7/8 • 96 pages color throughout
SZ • **$12.95**

SERGED GARMENTS IN MINUTES
by Tammy Young and Naomi Baker
Discover a progressive approach to creating beautiful fashions in less than an hour! Serge your way to complete garment construction. Master the basics of serging and learn to add finishing treatments and serge specialty fabrics in a matter of minutes.
Softcover • 8-1/4 x 10-7/8
144 pages • 8-page color section
SGIM • **$16.95**

GARMENTS WITH STYLE
Adding Flair to Tops, Jackets, Vests, Dresses, and More
by Mary Mulari
First there was the sweatshirt: plain, basic, comfortable! Then, Mary Mulari came along and suddenly everybody's favorite garment had pizzazz, style, even class! More than 100 individual projects with clear, concise directions.
Softcover • 8-1/4 x 10-7/8
144 pages • color throughout
GWS • **$17.95**

JAN SAUNDERS' WARDROBE QUICK-FIXES
How to Lengthen/Shorten, Loosen/Tighten, Update, Embellish, Repair, and Care for Your Clothing
by Jan Saunders
This is the one sewing book you mustn't be without! Complete instructions for all sewing levels will help you fix clothes in an emergency or create beautiful wardrobes at your leisure. Even includes time-saving no-sew techniques.
Softcover • 8-1/4 x 10-7/8 • 176 pages color throughout
WQF • **$14.95**